Ticket
to Ride

Ticket
to Ride
PETER LAMPL

HANNCKE,

BEST WISHES

PETER

HarperCollins*Publishers*

HarperCollins*Publishers*
1 London Bridge Street
London SE1 9GF

www.harpercollins.co.uk

HarperCollins*Publishers*
1st Floor, Watermarque Building, Ringsend Road
Dublin 4, Ireland

First published by HarperCollins*Publishers* 2021

1 3 5 7 9 10 8 6 4 2

© Sir Peter Lampl 2021

Sir Peter Lampl asserts the moral right to
be identified as the author of this work

A catalogue record of this book is
available from the British Library

ISBN 978-0-00-837238-5

Printed and bound in Great Britain by
CPI Group (UK) Ltd, Croydon

MIX
Paper from
responsible sources
FSC
www.fsc.org **FSC™ C007454**

This book is produced from independently certified FSC™ paper
to ensure responsible forest management

For more information visit: www.harpercollins.co.uk/green

For Fred and Margaret,
my parents

For Susan,
my wife

And for Katie, Chris and Steph,
my children

CONTENTS

Introduction   ix

1 On the Brink   1

2 Setting Up Home   17

3 Ticket to Ride   36

4 On Trial in Oxford   53

5 Confessions of a Drug Dealer   72

6 Getting Down to Business   81

7 Cash Cows and Question Marks   94

8 Seeing the Wood for the Trees   110

9   Making Some Money   127

10 Making Some More Money   148

11 Dunblane and After   161

12 Back to School (and Back to College)   179

13 Open Access   206

14 Socially Mobile   221

15 My Vanishing Act. And My Reappearing Act   242

16 Entrepreneurial Philanthropy for All   252

    Afterword   263

    Acknowledgements   271

INTRODUCTION

'The only way *you'll* go to Oxford is on the bus.'

That's what my physics teacher told me when I was 17. It was a good line, and Coot, as we called him (on account of the fact that he was completely bald, and on account of the fact that we were schoolboys), seemed to enjoy delivering it.

In fairness to Coot, I possibly didn't look much like Oxford material. I was newly arrived at the school, halfway through the A level course, a bit lost, and proposing to do a degree in a subject that I had failed at O level.

I did go to Oxford, though, and not just on the bus. And if that startled Coot, I don't like to think how he might have reacted in 2014 when the college where I had been a student named a building after me.*

---

* The Lampl Building. It's a student accommodation block. And no, before you ask, I didn't pay for it. The first I knew about it was when the President rang up and said they were doing it. It was a very nice surprise. Corpus had already awarded me an honorary fellowship. Again, I didn't turn up my nose.

It would also have been interesting to get a view from Coot when I turned up on a list of the '50 wisest people in Britain'. Mind you, that one surprised me as well. There I was alongside Tim Berners-Lee, the inventor of the World Wide Web, Francis Crick, who discovered the DNA double-helix, and Sir Bob Geldof, who wrote 'I Don't Like Mondays' for the Boomtown Rats.

'We are looking for people who have been around and done things that have made them wise,' explained someone involved with drawing up the list, which appeared in *Saga* magazine. 'We don't pretend it's the perfect list,' they added.

Ah.

Still, you might wonder what had I done to have a building in Oxford named after me and to get lumped in, however imperfectly, with Francis Crick (and also, incidentally, the historian Simon Schama and the Queen)?

Well, I had earned myself a reputation over two decades as 'the UK's leading educational philanthropist'. The first time I saw that in print I thought it sounded pretty grand. Then I realized I couldn't think of another one.

But first I was an entrepreneur who started a company which acquired underperforming businesses and managed them into profitability. Between 1987 and 1997, I made over £100 million which would be worth £230 million in today's money. I bought some nice properties and some nice cars and played golf on some nice courses before starting to wonder whether there was something more useful I could be doing with my money.

My dad was a Viennese refugee who arrived in England barely knowing any English. I grew up on a council estate in Yorkshire until I was eleven. But Britain in those days was still a place where the system offered opportunities to bright kids from poor backgrounds – chances you could seize to improve your lot and succeed. My dad seized those chances, and so did I. Of course, you would still need luck. But at least you could give yourself a chance to get lucky.

Then I came back to the UK after 20 years living in the States, and Britain didn't look like that anymore. The kind of education that I had benefitted from was still available, but not to kids like me. It had become the preserve of the wealthy. Doors had closed. Social mobility had stalled. The rich were OK (and more than OK), but the poor were increasingly adrift. The machinery had seized up. Britain was a country where your chances of coming from nowhere and ending up somewhere, as I had done, were vanishing alarmingly.

In the wake of the Dunblane primary school shooting on 13 March 1996, I ended up funding the anti-handgun campaign and thinking hard about philanthropy. Then I put business aside and set up and ran the Sutton Trust to give low- and moderate-income kids the opportunity to change their lives and to agitate for greater social mobility.

This book tells the story of all that – my adventures in making money and giving it away. Those adventures take place on a journey extending from Yorkshire to Seattle and from Chicago to Munich, with many points in between. In the pages that follow, I'll revisit New York in the dollar-mad 1980s, the buccaneering early days of leveraged buy-outs, and explain how I got caught up in a family turf war while innocently trying to buy a bankrupt wood products company. I'll travel to America's Deep South and try to unpack the fine art of buying a company from someone with a loaded shotgun leaning against his desk. Back in London, I'll explore the pros and cons of living next door to Margaret Thatcher and examine the 48 hours I spent on the police's missing persons list. And over in Germany, I'll explain why, when the Berlin Wall came down, it was a good time to be invested in building materials.

And I'll describe the building of the Sutton Trust and how we went about changing the future for tens of thousands of bright kids from low-income backgrounds, directly influencing government policy and putting social mobility at the heart of the national conversation.

Finally, I'll come to consider what philanthropy actually means, why British people do so little of it, and how it lies within the grasp of practically every one of us, not just the wealthy, to be an entrepreneurial philanthropist and make the world a little fairer.

Because if there's one thing I've learned over the course of my life as an entrepreneur, it's that people can surprise you, if they only get the chance.

Just ask Coot.

1

ON THE BRINK

Allow me to offer you a solid-gold business tip: in a high-stakes deal, when push is coming to shove and the future of your entire company is on the line, never underestimate the value of windsurfing.

It was September 1984 and I had flown to Seattle to try and persuade the president of the biggest privately owned forestry products company in America to sell me part of his business. To say I had a keen interest in clinching this deal would be putting it mildly. Twenty-one months previously I had quit my job as president of International Paper Realty in New York. That was a good, handsomely paid executive position in a huge company: at the time International Paper were the largest private landowners in the world, with vast holdings – 8.5 million acres, roughly equivalent to the area of Massachusetts and Connecticut combined. I had been head-hunted to work for International Paper from the Boston Consulting Group, which I had joined after graduating from London Business School. BCG were the world's leading management consulting firm, but after four years of consulting I wanted to get some hands-on general management experience under my belt. International Paper certainly provided it. I was responsible for the company's timberland deals (we were by far the biggest player in the North American market) and property developments, in which role I spent a fair amount of time flying around America looking at golf and ski-resort developments. There are worse jobs.

Yet I was ambitious and restless, with a strong entrepreneurial streak, and I yearned for independence and the chance to build something of my own. So, aged 35, I left my job and all its comforts and certainties, and set up on my own, ploughing some money I had saved into founding what I christened the Sutton Company,* with a smart Manhattan office on 45th and Third Street – its balcony offering a wonderful view of the Chrysler Building – and a plan to do deals in what had become my area of expertise, timberlands.

However, in the 21 months since foundation, the total number of acquisitions the Sutton Company – this bold

---

* Why the Sutton Company? I thought long and hard about that name. I reckoned I needed something that sounded transatlantic, plausible, classy yet innocuous … and that wasn't my name, in case the business went belly up and took my name down with it. I happened to be living on Beekman Place in New York, which is very close to Sutton Place. That chimed with me, because when I was a schoolboy in Reigate in Surrey, I lived quite near Sutton. An obscure coincidence? Obviously. But to me, with a company to name, it felt too good to ignore. The Sutton Company it was.

new break-away venture of mine – had successfully landed could be calculated very quickly: none.

Which is to say, none whatsoever. Zero.

This was not for the want of trying. On the contrary, since the company's inception, I had spent practically every waking hour hunting down and scrutinizing plausible projects, and I had got a long way down the line with a couple of them. But thus far my best efforts to close a deal had fallen victim variously to bad luck, bad timing, other people's unscrupulous practices and even a sudden and unforeseen outbreak of New York family warfare.

There was, for instance, the deal I got involved in with the American industrialist Peter M. Brant, a piece of business which had looked promising when I embarked upon it, but, alas, quickly devolved into a long and winding lawsuit.

Brant was one of those high-living characters that the eighties American business world seemed to throw out in unusual quantities – the kind of person who commissions Andy Warhol to paint their cocker spaniel.* As well as art and spaniels, Brant was absorbed by polo, which he played to a high standard, and he had stakes in racehorses, including the famous Swale, which won the Kentucky Derby and Belmont Stakes in the same year (1984) and then mysteriously collapsed and died eight days later. The walls of Brant's office in Greenwich, Connecticut, were practically papered with photos of him standing next to a horse which

---

* Brant actually did this. I'm not kidding.

had just won a 'Stakes race', as he would proudly tell you. He was also the owner of Conyers Farm, an enormously covetable tract of land in Greenwich, Connecticut, which he had converted into high-end residential where people like tennis player Ivan Lendl and actor Tom Cruise had homes.

Growing up in Queens, Brant had been the schoolboy pal of a certain Donald J. Trump. Apparently Brant and the future 45th President of the United States would sometimes venture into Manhattan together on Saturdays and stock up on stink bombs and fake vomit at a novelty store. Some would say they retained a fair bit in common beyond those days. Both were the privileged sons of successful business-men and both possessed an unashamed brashness and a certain willingness to cut corners and nudge the boundaries both at work and at play. I once had the pleasure of playing Brant at squash. (In the eighties, the squash court was argu-ably second only to the golf course as the recreational space in which business got done.) I'm not saying the guy cheated exactly, but there was an awful lot of 'accidental interfer-ence' in the course of our rallies and a suspiciously high number of lets. In due course, Brant would try nudging the boundaries of fair play with the IRS, which would not turn out so well. He was eventually sentenced to three months in jail for tax evasion.

But at this point, that particular twist in the story still lay ahead. In the early eighties, when I became involved with him, Brant had successfully expanded his father's news-print business, Brant-Allen Industries, and was an extremely important player in that area. One of his newsprint mills,

4

acquired in partnership with the *Washington Post*, was in Ashland, Virginia, and Brant was looking to buy some additional timberland around it to guarantee more independent supply.

Which is where I came in, with my brand-new Sutton Company. Why would Brant be interested in partnering with me and my as yet unproven start-up? Well, I had my reputation in this area, after those years at International Paper. I also had thick, cream, headed notepaper – the most sumptuous headed notepaper I could find. I had the notepaper for the same reason I had the smart office with a balcony on 45th Street: because appearances matter. They always have, and they always will, but in the ultra-showy eighties, they possibly mattered even more than usual. I certainly at that time didn't want anyone thinking I was running some kind of low-budget, amateur, kitchen-table operation. I remember Brant running his fingers over a sheet of luscious Sutton Company stationery and saying, 'My God, this stuff would make a schoolboy smile on a Monday morning.'

In collaboration with Brant, I went to work, helping strike the terms for a deal to acquire the desired additional timberland around the Ashland mill. Brant and I eventually travelled to Washington and I attended a meeting in the *Washington Post*'s boardroom with the *Post*'s legendary chairwoman, Katharine Graham, where the company approved the purchase. Everything was flying. I stood to earn a percentage of the deal. By my calculations, the Sutton Company would make at least half a million dollars.

It was soon after this, though, that Brant and I found ourselves somewhat at variance over the nature of our relationship. With the deal concluded, he began to imply that my role all along had been merely as a consultant. This apparent change of heart, and Brant's seeming determination to stand by it, caused me reluctantly to bring in a lawyer.

At the deposition, Brant gave no indication that he was particularly pleased to be there, or that he was taking the matter especially seriously. At some point in our dealings, I had made the mistake of addressing a letter to 'Peter Brandt', inserting a 'd', because when I heard the name 'Brandt' in those days, I automatically thought of the German Chancellor, Willy Brandt.*

This now came back to haunt me. 'You can't even spell my name!' he bellowed. He also seemed highly inclined to wave our claim away. 'Ah, he's just trying to make money out of me,' he said at one point.

To which my lawyer rather pointedly replied: 'Mr Brant, some of us have to make a living.'

The best moment of all came when we pointed out that we had evidence of payments to us from Brant indicating someone working on a success fee basis, which was higher than the kind of fee that might be paid to a consultant. Brant's explanation for this discrepancy was as follows: 'It's like when you're having your shoes shined. You give

---

* Willy Brandt (1913–92), Chancellor of the Federal Republic of Germany between 1969 and 1974.

the guy a buck, and if you think he's done a good job, you give him a buck more.'

Neither I nor my lawyer was particularly satisfied by this argument, and although I was pleased to hear that Brant thought I had been doing a good job, I didn't relish the implication that I was some kind of shoeshine boy. Do shoeshine boys have high-quality thick cream notepaper? I think not.

Anyway, none of this was making the Sutton Company any richer. The case rumbled on, and, at the point at which I flew into Seattle, wouldn't be resolved for another four years.*

Then, even more dispiritingly, there was the situation I had got into while attempting to buy a bankrupt treated wood company in New York State. This was low-hanging fruit, maybe. Certainly when I founded the Sutton Company I had been setting my sights a little higher than offcuts left on the floors of the bankruptcy courts. But I definitely saw some potential in this particular business. Once again, it was in an area that I understood. I had looked at it very closely and I was confident that I could manage the business back onto its feet and turn it around. What's more (and this was definitely attractive), I was, so far as I understood, the only buyer in the frame.

My friend Charlie Evans put together a crucial piece of the financing. The bank EF Hutton, now defunct, were

---

* Brant eventually agreed to pay me $300,000. Which wasn't $500,000, but wasn't bad.

persuaded to put up the rest. The treated wood company, by the way, was called Dutton. So we had Sutton buying Dutton with financing from Hutton. Sutton, Dutton, Hutton … We seemed to be arranging a bankruptcy buy-out and writing a Roald Dahl children's story at the same time.

Still, we had done all the painstaking prep work. Everything was in place – the price was agreed with the seller, the contracts were drawn up, the bank financing was there – and the only hurdle that remained was the obligatory court hearing at which the sale would be officially approved.

On the appointed date, Charlie and I drove out to the unromantic destination of Poughkeepsie in the Hudson Valley to complete the formalities, fully expecting to see the judge bang the gavel – or at least bring down the ink-stamp – and hand us the paperwork. Finally the Sutton Company was going to own something.

To lend the moment the grandeur it clearly merited, I rented a Cadillac for our 140-mile round-trip – a giant black whale of an automobile. Appearances again: I wanted to turn up in style and look like we had some money, and on this occasion a compact simply wasn't going to cut it. The rented Caddy was suitably large and imposing. Unfortunately, as I discovered when I got behind the wheel, it was also a complete lemon. The suspension was shot and it was all I could do to keep the car's massive frame on the road in a straight line. Charlie and I bounced up the Taconic State Parkway as though we were riding a rubber ball.

Consequently we were both pretty queasy by the time we walked into that drab New York State court room. We were also immediately mystified to discover a number of other people already present – two clusters of them, to be exact, on opposite sides of the room. Spectators? Apparently not. The judge began the proceedings and formally declared our agreed price for the company. At that point, a voice piped up from the left-hand corner of the room and made a counter-offer, slightly higher than ours.

This was not in the script. Charlie and I looked at each other in astonishment, then quickly scrambled together our response. There was a small amount of slack in our bid. We put in a counter-offer to the counter-offer. Without hesitation, the voice from the left-hand corner of the room piped up again, lodging another bid.

The judge now looked at us expectantly. It seemed an impromptu auction was under way.

Charlie and I conferred again, then lodged another offer. Back came the left-hand side of the room.

This went on for a few minutes until our carefully prepared bid was in shreds. We couldn't go any higher. We were out. We held our hands up in sad surrender and began to gather together our things. At which point a *third* voice piped up, this time from the right-hand side of the room. And off the auction went again, left side against right side now, the price rising higher and higher. Charlie and I sat open-mouthed between these mystery bidders, our heads swivelling from side to side as if we were watching a game of tennis. Meanwhile the price of the busted company soared ridiculously skywards.

Still the auction went on, and still the price rose. Eventually, thoroughly dejected, we put on our coats and left them to it.

Back in Manhattan, after a long, largely silent and annoyingly bouncy drive home in the terrible rented Caddy, we stopped in at Charlie's apartment, where we were greeted by his wife, Kathy, in a state of excitement.

'Charlie! Charlie! What happened?'

Charlie pulled the pockets out of his trousers and said mournfully, with his slow Arkansas drawl, 'Kathy, we just ran out of money.'

The next morning, still deflated, I got into the office at 7 a.m. and at 7.30 the phone rang. It was the victorious bidder.

'Why would you be calling me now?' I said.

It turned out that the guy didn't really want the company at all; he simply hadn't wanted the people on the other side of the room to have it. Apparently Charlie and I had inadvertently got caught in the middle of a turf war between two long-established and bitterly opposed New York families. Unbeknown to us, the tennis match we had been watching in that Poughkeepsie court room was Hudson Valley v. Long Island. The Hudson Valley guys' sole purpose was to keep the Long Island guys off their patch. Having triumphantly accomplished that mission, Team Hudson Valley had woken up bright and early to find themselves the owners of a bankrupt treated wood company for which they had no real use or desire. So, my caller's question, at 7.30 in the morning, was: would I like to take the thing off his hands?

'Well, sure – but for how much?'

He quoted a price so high, and so far beyond our means, that I would have honked with laughter if I hadn't been so close to screaming with frustration.

So, game over. Another fresh-air shot. More wasted motion for the Sutton Company. Thousands of dollars burned in legal fees and bank charges, and nothing to show for it. Add that to 21 months of rent on a plush midtown office which had started to look a touch hubristic and 21 months of salary for a secretary, plus a pricey ongoing legal case ticking away in the background. Not to mention the cost of the notepaper. As the savings drained away, in order to keep the company floating, I had sold my New York apartment on Beekman Place and moved into a rental. Now I put a second mortgage on my house on Long Island. The clock was officially running down. If something didn't come good soon, the Sutton Company would be winding up before it had really started, my dreams of independent entrepreneurship would be in tatters and I would be slinking away from the wreckage with my tail between my legs.

This, then, was the state of play when my flight from New York landed in Seattle that afternoon in 1984. It was one last roll of the dice, frankly, although, for obvious strategic reasons, I wasn't going to let it appear to be so. I was there to try and strike a deal with a man called Furman Moseley, who was president of the Simpson Timber

Company, a huge American forest products concern dealing in timberland, pulp, paper and corrugated packaging. The part of the business that I wanted to buy was a distribution company supplying building materials to the trade. It represented a negligible fraction of the vast Simpson empire, in truth. The company was haemorrhaging money and Simpson wanted to get shot of it. But, once again, the business was in an area that I knew something about, and it was a distribution company, which I liked because it's easy to make changes to distribution companies. I had done the research, looked into the background very thoroughly, and thought I saw something there that I could turn around.

I had initially been alerted to the sale by Donald P. Brennan, a man to whom my career owes a lot. A tough Irish-American who could scare the life out of people and rather enjoyed doing so, Brennan had been my boss at International Paper and had then taken up a post heading merchant banking at Morgan Stanley. He would occasionally call up and toss me bits and pieces – sales that had come across his desk that Morgan Stanley had no interest in. Referrals are, of course, priceless. It was because Donald Brennan had spoken up for me that Furman Moseley had agreed to see me.

Moseley picked me up at the airport in person, driving a huge SUV. He was a large, outdoorsy man, the kind of guy you could imagine spending his weekends in a plaid shirt, hiking and camping and standing photogenically on ridges with his eyes on the far horizon and his hand robustly on his knee. It was hard not to feel a little small and pallid in his presence, especially when you were just off a six-hour flight from New York. But he was warm and welcoming and suggested that instead of going to a restaurant, he should drive us straight out to his family home, which was on a private estate in the super-rich Medina neighbourhood of Seattle on the edge of Lake Washington. (Bill Gates and Jeff Bezos live round those parts now. That's how super-rich the neighbourhood is.)

When we arrived, I tried not to gasp at the scale of the property: the well-appointed mansion, the manicured grounds, the broad water-frontage. I had never seen anything quite like it. It was September and a storm was brewing. Moseley suggested we went down to the shoreline and had a look at the lake while we could. Lightning was already flickering on the skyline, thunder was rumbling in the distance and a gathering wind was making the lake look choppy.

That was when I noticed the windsurfing board lying idle near the water.

'Wouldn't it be great to go out on the lake?'

Moseley gave me a look as if to say 'What kind of idiot …?'

'Are you serious? In this weather?'

Suddenly I was. One problem, though: no swimming kit. I had arrived from New York in a suit and tie for a business dinner. I certainly hadn't packed for water sports.

Not a problem. From somewhere on the property, a pair of swimming shorts was conjured up. They belonged to

Moseley. They were bright yellow. This did not concern me. They were also, at a rough initial estimate, three sizes too big for me. This concerned me more. Still, better than nothing. I changed and re-emerged in the outsized trunks.

By this point my host had been joined on the shore by his daughter, who was no doubt curious to see this naïve visiting businessman either get fried by lightning or resoundingly dunked in the lake, or possibly, if she was really lucky, both at the same time.

Undeterred, and with as confident a stride as it was possible to muster in a pair of bright yellow shorts that were three sizes too big for me, I took the board down to the water, waded out a short way and then climbed onto it.

Sadly, no footage exists of my efforts on Lake Washington that day. So you will just have to take my word that what ensued was a classic battle between man, the elements and a pair of outsized swimming trunks. Looking back, it's hard to assess which was the greater of the twin challenges that I faced out there: keeping the sail out of the water or keeping the shorts up. I can only report that the water chopped, the board bucked, the thunder boomed and the shorts slipped ever lower. Yet by adopting an extra-wide stance and employing the extraordinary force of will-power, I somehow managed an entirely upright stint on the water without at any point spoiling the effect by exposing myself either to my hosts or to anyone else in Seattle's highly desirable Medina district.

I returned in triumph to find Moseley hooting with laughter and shouting his congratulations. Had this impromptu excursion on the water altered the dynamic between us? I'll just say this: I changed back into my suit, we returned to the house for a barbecue and then withdrew to Moseley's study, where I made an outrageous offer for the company which, much to my amazement, Moseley happily accepted and the pair of us shook hands on the deal.

Now, had I mentioned to my host at any point that I was an experienced windsurfer who had competed in the 1982 North American Championships in Cancun, Mexico? Maybe I would save that little tale for later in the day (just as I will save it for later in this book). In the meantime, I would spend a little more time enjoying my new reputation as a plucky, devil-may-care hero, while simultaneously relishing my relief that finally the Sutton Company had managed to buy something.

Two and a half years later, having made another acquisition in the same industry, I sold the combined entity, generating $18 million after paying back debt. These two acquisitions were the first of 13 completed by the Sutton Company over the next decade that would net $180 million.*

These deals would see me amass a personal fortune on a scale that would have seemed unlikely when I landed in Seattle that day in 1984. And it certainly would not have

* Just to lend some contemporary perspective here, $18 million in 1987 would be the equivalent of £34 million in 2020. That's not chump change. And $180 million in 1997 would be the equivalent of £230 million in 2020. That's not chump change, either.

appeared to be on the cards when, just a few months old, I arrived from Vienna with my parents to live with my grandparents in a modest terraced house in Batley, Yorkshire.

2

SETTING UP HOME

I was born on 21 May 1947 at the Rudolfsheim Hospital in Vienna and, frankly, the city had looked a lot better. Two years earlier, when the Second World War had ended, Austria's capital had taken a battering from all sides of the conflict. The liberating Russians hit the place from the outside with tank artillery, and the occupying Germans went out with a bang by carefully destroying as many bridges over the Danube as they could. Meanwhile the Allied bombers rained havoc down from the skies, contributing to the destruction of a fifth of the city's houses. Vienna would be a while recovering.

Not that I hung around to see it do so. Vienna was a mess, divided into four zones, just like Berlin: French, British, Russian and American. These days, you will routinely find the city ranked top or thereabouts in the various annual 'world's most liveable cities' surveys. Not then. The place was a disaster. There was no work; my father couldn't make a living. So within six months my parents – my Austrian father and my German mother – reluctantly gave up on it, packed up me and the rest of their belongings and traded Vienna for somewhere which, so far as I'm aware, has yet to trouble the 'world's most liveable cities' judges: Batley in Yorkshire.

This was where my father's parents had landed up after escaping to England in 1939 – a stern-looking textile manufacturing town, where my grandparents now generously handed over the top floor of their terraced house to their son, daughter-in-law and infant grandson. We were there until I was four.

Inevitably, my memories of those days are patchy. I chiefly remember the outside loo in the back yard and, for some reason, the silvery trails occasionally left by snails on the downstairs carpets. I also have an abiding memory of gritty, polluted air from the town's numerous smokestacks, although I may have added that by association later. What I know for sure is that my father, Fred, studied towards a Higher National Certificate in Engineering, while my mother, Margaret, patiently endured four years of that perhaps unparalleled form of domestic suffering: living with your in-laws.

At some point, it seems, we nearly upped and quit for New Zealand. My grandparents left Batley for Christchurch, with a view to setting up home there, and the plan was that we would follow them. However, my father was studying, my mother was pregnant with my sister … heading for the other side of the world very quickly came to look like a badly timed suggestion. So the plan was scrapped and my grandparents, who didn't want to be down in New Zealand on their own, returned to England.

The memories start to come more thickly after we left my grandparents' house and moved to Wakefield, seven miles away. Here we took up residence in a semi-detached single-storey house in a peaceful cul-de-sac on the Lupset council estate – 9 Gloucester Road, to be exact. Our new home was a pre-fab, put up to counter the huge post-war housing shortages, and probably only intended to do service for 20 years or so, although it's still standing. It was spanking new and very nicely appointed. It had its own front garden, a shiny and slippery tiled hallway floor, consistently polished to the condition of glass by my mother, a bathroom with (rejoice) an indoor loo and three bedrooms – one for my parents, one for me and one for my sister, Erica, who had now arrived. My father had taken a job as a draughtsman for a mining engineering firm. Once my sister and I were both at school, my mother went to work as a receptionist at a Wakefield doctor's surgery. All in all, we were pretty well set up.

Wakefield seemed to specialize in large council estates, but Lupset was the largest of them. It was socially quite mixed. There were a lot of blue-collar workers and their families, clearly, but there were also a number of young white-collar families. And there were definitely a few miners: I would see them coming home from their shifts, caked in coal dust. It was a good place to live – especially if you were a kid and liked having other kids to play with. There was never a shortage of those. There would always be a bunch of youngsters around who had been turned onto the streets to amuse themselves.

At the top of the cul-de-sac there was a patch of grass which was the perfect venue for pick-up games of football or cricket or rugby.* In the winter, when it snowed (which it seemed to do most years), the hill loaned itself perfectly to tobogganing. Well, it was perfect if you didn't mind the entirely blind corner at the bottom of the run. But what were the chances of a car coming? Slim enough that we were prepared to risk it over and over again.

There was also a big rubbish tip, out on the estate's perimeter, which offered a steady supply of rats for target practice. A friend had an air rifle and every now and again we would head off to the rubbish tip on safari. It turns out that if you want to take out a rat with a cheap plastic air rifle, you'll need to be a pretty good shot. We never managed it. But it didn't stop us trying. (No air rifle for me, by the way. No toy guns of any sort, in fact. My father wouldn't permit it. He had seen too many awful things in the war while holding a real one to feel comfortable with guns as playthings.)

If you wandered a bit further, you were out in the rhubarb fields. Wakefield, as I'm sure nobody will need reminding, is the rhubarb capital of the United Kingdom, and sits, with Morley and Rothwell, in the area known poetically as 'the Rhubarb Triangle' – no relation to the

---

* Rugby league, of course, this being Yorkshire – not the soft southern 'union' version of the game.

Bermuda Triangle, I should say, although there were so many rhubarb fields around that you could easily disappear into them for a while. All in all, I was given a very happy boyhood on the Lupset estate, where there was space to play in, where you roamed free and where nobody really bothered too much about where you were or what you were up to as long as you were home by six for your tea.

My school, Snapethorpe Primary, was on the estate, an easy, unaccompanied walk from our house, and rejoiced in its own sports field. I went back there three or four years ago and, unusually for a state school in England, it still has that field. In Snapethorpe's classrooms, I was taught to recite the rivers of Yorkshire from north to south in a broad Yorkshire accent. Yet I was growing up bilingual. At home we spoke German and English – sometimes in the same sentence. Similarly, my mother would cook excellent Viennese schnitzel and sauerkraut, but equally excellent fried bread or bangers and mash. So we were a proper Austro-German-English mix, I guess. Were we outsiders? It didn't much feel like it to me. We supported the local rugby league team, the mighty Wakefield Trinity, swathed in scarves like everyone else. I suppose there was something unavoidably 'different' about us in the context of a Yorkshire council estate, and we certainly had an unusual surname among the Lunns and Warmsleys and Newsomes, but I don't ever recall this difference being used against me by my peers. I was gregarious, I played sport, I made friends. And in this I seemed to follow the lead of my parents, who appeared to fit in easily. They were a charming couple, which helped. Good-looking, too.

It must also have been to their advantage that my father was a person who could mend things. He was a smart man, and an enormously practical one. Word soon got around about this. People on the estate were beginning to have their own cars. And because this was the 1950s, those cars were always breaking down or proving difficult to start. Consequently there was a steady stream of people at the door asking for Fred, wondering if he would mind having a look at the motor. Scuffing my way up the street on the way home from the playground or the rubbish tip or the rhubarb fields, I was forever seeing a pair of overalled legs protruding from underneath a Morris Minor at the kerbside and realizing that they belonged to my father.

In the evenings, once the table was cleared and the washing up was done, my father taught me to play chess on the kitchen table, and he taught me to play it well, because he didn't think there was much point doing something if you weren't going to do it properly. As a consequence, by the age of ten, I had a bit of a reputation at Snapethorpe as the resident chess whizz, to the point where teachers thought it was fun to take me on during break or the lunch hour. This didn't make me very happy: I wanted to be out and running around on the playground. It didn't play well with my peers, either. 'Where's Peter?' 'He's playing chess against Mr Jones.' That's not the kind of thing to burnish your reputation as a happening kind of guy. I felt a bit like a chess version of the Elephant Man: 'Here's this freak – he'll beat you at chess.' I usually did, mind you.

One day Snapethorpe was visited for a chess match by Queen Elizabeth's Grammar School, known to all as QUEGS, a private school with grand if rather austere premises in Northgate, and patronized by Wakefield's well-off. I was drawn to play against a QUEGS boy who immediately and unsentimentally began dismantling me on the board. The effect of this on my youthful self was utterly harrowing. It was a trouncing such as I had never experienced. I'm afraid I was a terrible loser in those days – the kind who wept when things didn't quite go the right way for him on the Monopoly board. But this seemed to be something extra – something even worse than the uniquely shrivelling experience of getting soundly whipped at chess.

A few weeks later, still feeling haunted, I headed over to QUEGS' well-appointed halls for the return leg, where the same guy awaited. There was already enough riding on this re-match from my point of view, but just to make the stakes even higher, whichever of us triumphed that afternoon would go on to represent our region at the national schools chess championships in London – a giddy honour. Following our first encounter, it seemed pretty obvious which way the wind was going to blow. And yet what do you know? It was *Rocky* all over again, except, obviously, with chess pieces. The plucky downtrodden contender from the wrong side of town pulled himself up onto his feet, dragged himself back into the ring and, with the desire for revenge and glory coursing through his system, beat his former nemesis.

Now, I don't want to overstate the impact of a solitary and insignificant school chess match on the subsequent course of my life – perish the thought. Yet, my God, that felt good.

In the Hollywood version of this story, fresh from this triumph and with confidence surging, I head off down to London in a cloud of glory and become the youngest Yorkshire schoolboy ever to win the national championships. Alas, not quite. I caught the train with my mother – my first trip to the capital – and headed over to the exhibition centre at Earl's Court, where, amid scenes of thinly disguised chaos, a crowd seemingly in the vicinity of 4 million schoolchildren were simultaneously playing chess around 2 million chess boards. I was used to far smaller, quieter places. I was also used to playing chess in the relatively leisurely 'against the clock' format. But the format for this Earl's Court competition was lightning chess, where you make your moves every 10 seconds, and I was all over the place. I got belted all around the room and trudged back to the railway station in a sombre mood. Ah well. I would always have QUEGS.

Even more than becoming a chess grandmaster, I think my father hoped that I would follow him into engineering. He plied me with Meccano building sets, with their nuts and bolts and metal struts, hoping to see my face come alight like the faces of the delighted children on the boxes. I was destined to be a disappointment to him in that regard.

Meccano didn't appeal to me at all. It became a battle-ground between us for a while – my father pressing, me resisting. So did Bayko, the plastic building kit from which you could fashion highly detailed model houses. This, too, my father dangled hopefully in front of me – the fiddly bits of plastic, the rods, the slots, the tabs … It wasn't for me.

I preferred to read a book: in German, Heinrich Hoffmann's *Struwwelpeter* and *Max und Moritz** by Wilhelm Busch; in English, Enid Blyton and Biggles books, borrowed from the school library. Best of all, there was Arthur Mee's *The Children's Encyclopaedia*. My parents didn't have many books in the house, but, with a view to Erica's and my improvement, they had bought the full ten volumes of this reference work and installed them neatly on a shelf in the front room. Those volumes seemed to me to be the fountain of all knowledge. I could reach up and pluck one down, open its section on 'Nature', say, or 'Wonder', or 'Great Lives', or 'Golden Deeds', and find myself transported to places that building an operational crane out of Meccano simply wasn't taking me.

Later, when I got into Oxford to read chemistry, my father consoled himself with the thought that although chemistry obviously could never match engineering, it was at least a science, and difficult. He was definitely proud of me, although I think he had mixed feelings for a while

---

* To give it its full name, *Max und Moritz: Eine Bubengeschichte in Sieben Streichen*, or *Max and Moritz: A Story of Seven Boyish Pranks*. It was written in rhyming couplets and loses a lot in translation.

about the way I had accelerated past him in terms of academic attainment with, as he saw it, such ease. He felt that, in comparison with him, I'd had it easy.

He certainly wasn't wrong about that.

Lampl family legend states that shortly after the First World War, my grandmother plonked a baby down firmly on the desk of the housing officer for the Fourteenth District of Vienna and forcefully demanded that her family be given somewhere to live.* Perfectly on cue, the baby began to wail uncontrollably, and the startled housing officer quickly found my grandparents and my crying infant father a second-storey apartment on Jadengasse, two blocks away from the railway line.

My father's family was from Jankowitz, which is now in Moravia in the eastern part of the Czech Republic, but in the late nineteenth century was a German-speaking part of the Austro-Hungarian Empire. My great-grandfather, Jakob Lampl, was a tailor who moved the family to Vienna in search of work. My grandfather in turn found a job with a Vienna-based international shipping firm, so, in a time of high unemployment, he was better placed than many. He

---

* I draw this recollection, and much of the material that follows here, from the short but highly detailed memoir of his early years that my father wrote and printed for distribution among the family. 'I feel that you should know more about the Lampl side of your family,' he began, 'and for this reason I am setting down the facts I still can remember and the impressions I have retained of my early life.' Without this memoir, the Lampl family history and the details of my father's life would be lost forever. It's a major reason why I decided to write a memoir.

was Jewish by birth, which is not to say he was of the Jewish faith. I don't believe my grandfather ever set foot in a synagogue. Yet at this terrifying moment in history, ethnicity was all that mattered. In 1938 my father was one year short of matriculation from the Gymnasium and looking ahead to university when the German army rolled, unopposed, into Austria.

Some Austrians genuinely welcomed the Nazis, believing that life was about to improve; others welcomed them because they knew better than to dissent at this point, the consequences of dissenting having been made clear to them. Either way, the German troops were met on their way into Vienna by cheering, flag-waving crowds and by windows festooned with *Hakenkreuzen* – swastikas.

My Catholic great-uncle on my grandmother's side, Leopold, was a seller of pots and pans who spotted a profitable emerging market in Nazi insignia and quickly commissioned a large batch of cloth badges from a local manufacturer. He then dragooned his little nephew, my father, into helping him hawk those badges on the local markets. If my father had been identified as half-Jewish during this commercial mission, who knows what might have happened to him. Luckily for him, he did not look at all Jewish.

It's withering to think about what my father knew and saw during his schoolboy days, and how short a span of time separates us from that period in history and its atrocities – the mere span, in fact, of one man's life. When Adolf Hitler stood on the balcony of Vienna's Hofburg

Palace and addressed the crowd in Heldenplatz, my father was there. He witnessed public speeches at rallies on the Ringstrasse by Joseph Goebbels, the Reich Minister of Propaganda, and Hermann Göring, the commander-in-chief of the Luftwaffe – heard them expertly stir the public against the so-called enemies within: communists, gypsies, foreigners and Jews. My father, who, at the time of writing, is still alive, aged 100, witnessed these things. And then he felt their impact.

A few days after the Anschluss, when Austria was annexed by Nazi Germany, my father and the four pupils from Jewish backgrounds in his class of 30 at the Gymnasium were separated from the rest of the children and seated on their own. They were then ostracized by their fellow students and ignored even by some of the teachers. My grandparents quickly withdrew my father from the school. But that cold trauma of being, as a 17-year-old, abruptly cast out by his former schoolfriends, for no reason that he could understand and for nothing that he could change, would live with him. I have never seen him become more upset than when recounting it.

Yet this was just the beginning. On account of being Jewish, my grandfather lost his job at the shipping firm. The fact that he had fought with the Austro-Hungarian army in the First World War appeared not to matter. The family of three were then evicted from their apartment. Their neighbour, with whom they had always been friendly, had joined the Nazi party and took over their rooms.

Clearly, exile was the only hope. My grandfather and father both queued for hours at overrun foreign consulates, seeking admission to other countries, only to be turned away. Venezuela looked promising for a while. Word was you could be given your own small slice of jungle down there, as long as you agreed to tend it. So one moment you were living as a family with a white-collar job in Vienna, the next you were seriously contemplating exile to a South American rainforest.

And then, to everyone's excitement, my grandfather managed to acquire tickets for a ferry from Bremen in Germany to somewhere closer than Venezuela – Lisbon in Portugal. The Portuguese borders were still open, so the family could plausibly move there and start over.

Come the day, my grandparents and father packed cases and boarded a train in Vienna. There followed a tense journey through Austria and Germany, with everybody worrying, every time the train stopped, that this was the moment they would be seized. Yet to everyone's relief, the train reached Bremen unhindered and everybody boarded the boat. A few days later, they docked in Lisbon – spared and now safe.

Their joy didn't last long. While the ship had been at sea, Portugal had closed its borders to refugees. Negotiations in the port came to nothing. All passengers were forced to remain on board and then sail on to Madeira. Here, everyone was transferred to a German cargo vessel on its way back from Argentina to Bremen. This devastating circular excursion took three weeks and ended with my grandparents and father back where they started in Vienna and more worried for their future than ever before.

Enough to go through an experience like that once in a lifetime. But my grandparents went through it twice. The second time, with renewed hope, they took a train to Stettin on the Baltic and then boarded a ferry for Riga in Estonia, only to be turned around on arrival and sent back to Germany.

Fortunately, just when all hope seemed gone, a visa arrived for my grandfather to do domestic work in England and the pair of them finally escaped, landing in England just a couple of months short of the outbreak of the war in 1939. Neither of them could speak a word of English, and neither had assumed their futures lay in domestic service, least of all my grandfather, who had until recently held a coveted white-collar job. But they had no option.

My father, meanwhile, had made his own escape. An application to the Society of Friends, a Quaker organization which had set up a rescue operation in Vienna, came good. The Society agreed to supply my father with a visa, transport to England and the offer of agricultural work. He could only speak the little English he had learned at school and had not planned on becoming a farm labourer. Here's this bright guy, doing really well, heading for university, and then this terrible thing happens and he ends up living in another country, milking cows. But again, there was no choice.

Now there was just the small matter of a nearly six-year global conflict to get through. As a guest of the Society of

Friends, my father was initially housed in a holiday camp at Lowestoft in Norfolk, which would arguably have been fairly testing at any time of the year, but was particularly so in December. He was then moved to Henley in Oxfordshire and given some training in basic farm work, and was relatively happily ensconced on a farm near Aldermaston in Berkshire when the police arrived in 1940 to intern him. At the outbreak of war in September 1939, 70,000 UK-dwelling Germans and Austrians were classified as enemy aliens, and he was one of them. He was transported initially to a temporary internment camp near Liverpool, where he claims to have enjoyed a meal of bread and raw herrings, and then transferred to Douglas on the Isle of Man, where he and his fellow Austrian internees lived 12 to a house.

A few months later he was among a group selected to sail to Canada. His boat, a Polish vessel, the *Sobieski*, broke down and idled for two days in the water while it was repaired and while my father and his fellow passengers nervously pondered the threat posed by German U-boats.*

Safely in Canada, my father was placed under guard in a camp surrounded by swampland near Ottawa, where the

---

* The threat was real. In July 1940, a few months before my father sailed, a British Blue Star Line cruise ship, the SS *Arandora Star*, was sunk by a German torpedo in the Atlantic, 75 miles west of the Irish coast. It was heading for Newfoundland, carrying 712 UK-based Italians and 438 UK-based Germans, including Jewish refugees. More than half of the passengers and crew lost their lives.

detainees were set to work building their own housing –
ten long wooden huts for 600 people. He was then given
some training as a lumberjack and sent into the forests to
chop down trees. All of which might sound gruelling, but
my father still has some good things to say about it. Coffee
and cake were available in the afternoons, apparently, and
there were inter-hut football tournaments, handball tournaments and, when the weather was right, even ice hockey
tournaments. My dad likes to say it would have been an
ideal holiday camp if it hadn't been for the wire fence.

Still, despite the allure of the cake and the handball and
the ice hockey, when the chance arose to be shipped back
to the UK and return to farm work, he jumped at it. Back
in England, he soon put farm labouring aside for a night-
shift job digging tunnels for the London Underground, and
after that he repaired cars at a garage near Hyde Park,
where he was able to swim in the Serpentine during his
lunch hours. Later he moved to a garage in less salubrious
Acton which specialized in lorry repairs, cycling the six
miles every morning from the flat he shared in Paddington
with some other Austrian exiles.

Meanwhile he had joined the Free Austria Movement –
an affiliation of young Austrians who were wedded to the
cause of defeating Hitler and returning to their country,
and who were also wedded, in the meantime, to organizing
dances and concerts and forming a football team, all of
which my father seems to have thrown himself into.

In November 1943, when Austrians in the UK were
granted permission to enlist in the British army, my father

was, literally, at the head of the queue. A picture in the London *Evening Standard* of the line outside the recruitment office showed him in a sports jacket and an open-neck shirt, with an eager expression on his face.* My grandfather had fought alongside the Germans in the First World War; now, 25 years later, my father was enlisting for the other side.

He was sent to the Maryhill barracks on the outskirts of Glasgow for basic infantry training, learning to manage ten miles of forced marching with a full pack on his back. And then he was moved to Suffolk to be schooled in the use of machine guns, hand grenades and anti-tank weapons. Training complete, he was shipped over to Holland with the Royal Scots Regiment under Field Marshal Montgomery and spent his first week on the front line lying in a shallow, wet trench holding a Bren gun. He went into battle near the River Maas in an open troop carrier with German bullets whistling over the top and thudding into its metal sides, and he threw himself over the side of that troop carrier into open fire. He fought in the Battle of the Bulge and crossed the Rhine in an uncovered amphibious vehicle under heavy artillery fire. Advancing through the Reichswald Forest to the Siegfried Line to relieve the British regiment, he picked his way through the bodies of massacred British soldiers, including a dispatch rider lying

* The photo was captioned: 'YOUNG AUSTRIANS CAN NOW JOIN THE BRITISH ARMY, and here is a queue of youthful members of the Free Austria Movement, waiting to enlist at a recruiting office today.'

headless beside his motorbike – a sight which would stay with him forever. Later, pressing on towards the River Elbe, he ran behind Churchill tanks which were exchanging fire with German Tigers and narrowly avoided death in a high-velocity German ambush on a seemingly secured village. In other words, he put his life on the line – and on at least three occasions came extremely close to losing it. He didn't have to do this. He *chose* to. I'm very proud of what he did in the war. He wasn't pushing paper across desks at a safe distance from the action. He was a fighting soldier for his time in the army – on the front line, getting shot at.

When the fighting was over, he was working as an interpreter for the British army in Bad Bramstedt in Germany, about 30 miles north of Hamburg – his fluency in German proving useful to him, just as one day, in very different circumstances, mine would prove useful to me. One weekend, he noticed a German girl at the outdoor swimming pool whom he especially liked the look of. In my father's telling (and he may be adding a sprinkling of myth here), he decided to use the trampoline beside the pool to pull off some handy moves in the hope of earning himself permission to walk this girl home. The moves worked and permission was granted – although it was almost retracted straight away when my father emerged from the changing cubicles in British army uniform. The war was over, but fraternizing with the other side was still entirely unacceptable. Utterly mortified, the girl would only let him walk her to the edge of her village.

Incidentally, as my father duly discovered, this girl's own wartime had not been uneventful. With her father in the German army and her mother and brother evacuated, she had lived on her own in the family home in Remscheid. An industrial town, the place was subject to heavy air raids and one night she took shelter, as usual, in the cellar. When the all-clear sounded and she emerged, the cellar was the only thing that remained of the house. The building had been completely wiped out and she was homeless, with no possessions. Shortly after this, recruited for the German war effort, she was sent to Hamburg and worked on the trams until the Allied bombing campaign ensured there were no Hamburg trams to work on.

But now here she was, in peacetime, in Bad Bramstedt, where she had been taken in by a friend, and gradually, as she grew to know my father, she became a little more willing to fraternize. My father and the German girl from the swimming pool, Margaret Assmann, got together, moved to Vienna and had me. My father stayed in the city long enough to complete the school matriculation that the German invasion in 1938 had denied him. And then they came to England, not even out of their twenties and yet already having seen and lived through more than their children would ever be able to fathom.

3

TICKET TO RIDE

I can still recite the register for my class at Reigate Grammar School, unhesitatingly and in alphabetical order, exactly as the form teacher called it out every morning. Want to hear me? Of course you don't.

Addison, Avernell, Barton, Black, Brown, Chapman …

This was Form PK, I should point out, which was short for Priory and Kinnersley, the names of two of the school's eight houses.

… Collins, Day, Ellice, Fisher, Gershon …

Gershon, by the way, was Sir Peter Gershon. He went on to become the chairman of Tate & Lyle and the National Grid and write the famous Gershon Review of public spending in 2004. He's now a trustee of the Sutton

Trust and on our board. So there were two future knights of the realm in this class, which I think would have surprised a few of the teachers, had you put it to them at the time.

… Goodhew, Hall, Holmwood, King …

These were the people I knocked around with from the age of 11 to 17 and in whose company I eventually sat O levels, almost all of us failing chemistry in a school-wide cock-up. Thanks to an oversight somewhere in the vicinity of the staffroom, we had been taught the wrong syllabus, so, come the day of the exam, we opened up the paper to find ourselves plunged into a world of science that was entirely new to us. Result: complete carnage.

… Lampl, Lawrence, Mann, Meade, Morris …

The business about screwing up chemistry wouldn't have mattered that much, except that somewhere along the way I had conceived a plan to study chemistry at university. So I was going to have to find a way around that.

… Palmer, Ransome, Russell, Stewart, Sweet, Taylor, Thom, Turner, Walters, Williams and Wright.

Which concludes my party piece. All 31 of them, form PK in full.

Now, if the party is going really well, I might be persuaded, for an encore, to reel off, in order, all the train stations in all four directions from Redhill. So, going west: Reigate, Betchworth, Deepdene, Dorking Town, Gomshall, Chilworth, Shalford, Guildford, Wanborough, Ash, North Camp, Farnborough North, Blackwater, Sandhurst Park, Wokingham and Reading.

But, as I say, that's only at the really swinging parties.

I have no idea why these details should be so firmly lodged in my memory. But they are. I suppose I did get to hear the teacher read out that roll-call many times over. And I suppose I did spend a fair amount of time on that train line, going one stop every morning from our new home in South Nutfield to Redhill, where I would catch a bus the rest of the way to Reigate and my new school. In 1959, with my father's career in engineering on the up, we had uprooted from Yorkshire and replanted ourselves in Surrey. My dad, who had qualified as a professional engineer, had a new job at Salford's near Horley, and I, who had passed my 11-plus exam, had a place at Reigate Grammar.

As an 11-year-old, I hadn't wanted to leave Lupset, but I could see that the move had its plus points. Our new house was detached – a kind of chalet-style place with Swiss wood on the front and half an acre of garden. For my parents, this was several steps up the social ladder from a council-owned pre-fab. South Nutfield also seemed to be leafier than Wakefield, and significantly warmer. Certainly the summer we moved was blazingly hot, and within walking distance of our house there was a public pool called the Wagon Shed, where I would go most days to swim, fool around and make new friends.

However, the thick Yorkshire accent that I had brought with me to Surrey appeared to be a hindrance. Nobody, from Addison and Avernell to Williams and Wright, seemed to be able to understand a word I said, and I was mercilessly tormented about it. 'What are you talking about?' they would ask. 'Say that again in English.' The combination of being a new arrival and 'speaking funny' made it hard for me to get accepted at first. I had to wrestle with that for a while.

In addition to speaking English differently, Addison, Avernell & co. seemed to have been doing Latin for a while. Classical languages hadn't much concerned us in those early years at Snapethorpe Primary. My dad, who had learned some Latin at the Gymnasium in Vienna, did his best to help me catch up at home. Somehow, though, when push came to shove, Latin held far less allure for me at school than sport, especially swimming. The school had its own pool, but it was outdoor and unheated, which meant that for about nine-tenths of the year, the water was cold enough to stun a polar bear. At some point near the end of the summer term the temperature would eventually crawl fractionally above freezing point, but the rest of the time you practically had to break pack-ice just to get in. One year the school magazine was obliged solemnly to report that the performances of the swimming team hadn't been quite as expected because the squad had lost *six weeks* of training to inhospitable conditions in the pool. Still, despite the cold, I was the fastest breaststroke swimmer in the school. Or perhaps the cold did have something to do with it. You didn't want to hang around in that water.

Rising, again, above the hostile health-and-safety environment represented by the facilities, I won the school diving, too. And I was a sometime member of the cross-country team. Frankly, with a view to establishing myself among my new peers, I was interested in pretty much any sport that was going, although I drew the line at rugby, which wasn't my idea of fun. I liked football better, but the school, with a degree of snobbery that was by no means exceptional among English grammars in the 1950s, considered 'soccer' to be a 'ruffians' game' and wouldn't allow it on the premises. So we played football outside school when the authorities weren't watching.

And there was chess, of course – though not for long. I had arrived in Surrey trailing clouds of glory as the hottest chess prodigy to come out of Wakefield since the last one. Now, boldly wearing on my Reigate uniform the chess badge awarded to me at Snapethorpe (because if you've got it, flaunt it, right?), I was fast-tracked into the Reigate Grammar team. Unfortunately, that team was drawn from right across the school, so at the age of 11, I found myself playing with, and against, kids as old as 18. This made the possibility of getting beaten in a withering manner by your intellectual superiors more than averagely likely. Some of these kids had really put some work into it, too, learning openings and special ways to play certain positions. The more casual, intuitive approach that had wowed the crowds back in Yorkshire was of no use to me here. Now, I was a competitive boy, clearly. But it seems I had that particular kind of competitiveness that makes you reluctant to expose yourself to situations where getting beaten is not just a possibility but a high likelihood. Certainly the pleasure of getting ritually outsmarted by gloating sixth-formers wore off pretty quickly. I played on for about a year, but after that the chess pieces went back in the cupboard and my glory years at the board were over.

By that time, I had settled into the school completely and my Yorkshire accent had softened and was on the way to vanishing completely. Within a handful of terms, by a process of immersion, I was pronouncing 'bath' to rhyme with 'hearth' along with everybody else.* I was happy and relaxed. Perhaps a bit too relaxed: school reports seemed to use the word 'lazy' quite a lot. I was keeping my head above water, though. And I was lucky in ways that I would only come to appreciate properly much later. With this move to Reigate, and the golden ticket of

---

* My accent underwent further upheaval during the 20 years I lived and worked in America, broadening a few vowels and losing a few consonants before eventually settling somewhere in the mid-Atlantic, where it continues to reside. Throughout these shifts, my German accent has, to the best of my knowledge, remained stable.

a place at its grammar school, my horizons had completely changed.

Late on in my time at Reigate, I made a good decision about the commercial viability of a new pop group from Liverpool called the Beatles. Yes, me and George Martin both, although I'll hand it to George: he got there first.

It was 1963 and, aged 15 going on 16, I was on the train home from school, idly leafing through a copy of the London *Evening Standard* which another passenger had left lying on a seat, when my eyes fell on an advertisement. In bold black letters, it said:

BRIAN EPSTEIN PRESENTS THE BEATLES CHRISTMAS SHOW.

The venue: Finsbury Park Astoria in London. Sixteen scheduled performances, from Christmas Eve through to 11 January.

Months away though it was, I figured that I might quite like to see that concert. I figured that a few other people might quite like to see it, too. Tickets were five shillings – pretty steep. On the other hand, thanks to a newspaper round and a couple of other sketchy weekend jobs, I had some capital salted away. So, back at home, I shook out the tin that contained my funds, calculated the sum total of my liquid assets, went to a post office, bought a postal order for £4 and sent off for, not one, not two, but 16 tickets to see the Beatles on New Year's Eve. And just like that, I was in business as a freelance Beatles ticket agent.

Now, with the advantage of hindsight, and knowing what we all do about Beatlemania in the sixties and the unparalleled magnetism of John, Paul, George and Ringo, this investment would hardly look like a massive gamble. Gold in a goldmine, frankly. Yet at the time, certainly to my teenage mind, it felt like quite a punt. Let's face it, who were the Beatles in the spring of 1963? They'd had a single out called 'Love Me Do', which had done modestly well, but which I'd found quite dull, if I'm being honest – a bit of a plodder. And then they'd released 'Please Please Me', which was much more like it, in my humble opinion. And indeed, it went to number one. But that was all we had to go on. Was this the stuff of which lasting greatness was made, or would it all be over by Christmas? Fame was fickle and, certainly in the early sixties, pop acts had the life expectancy of butterflies – another day, another 'next big thing'. Nobody knew how long the Beatles would last – including, I'm pretty sure, the Beatles.

So here was my hunch: that the Beatles of spring 1963 would still be a hot ticket come Christmas. Sure, they had only released two singles at this point, but I had heard enough to be sure of it. And if my hunch was wrong, the Beatle thing blew over before summer was out and you couldn't give the tickets away? Well, I could always go to the show with some mates. And have a seat or seven to put my coat on.

No such development, of course. In August the band

released 'She Loves You' – still, to my mind, the greatest track the Beatles ever recorded and a reliable burst of energy when you need it even now. The single roared up the charts on the back of unprecedented sales, the band appeared on *Sunday Night at the London Palladium*, cementing their legend across the UK, and by October Beatlemania was fully mainstream. Then, at the end of November, came 'I Wanna Hold Your Hand', the record that would start the fire for the band globally and that would have gone straight to number one in its first week if 'She Loves You' hadn't been in the way, meaning it had to wait for another fortnight. By that point, having a ticket for the Beatles, let alone in London and let alone on New Year's Eve, was like owning the Holy Grail. Sixteen copies of the Holy Grail, in my case.

Cultural foresight aside, I suppose I shouldn't be too proud of this youthful exercise in touting – or 'secondary ticketing', as we would now euphemistically call it. Still, I can't deny that I did it and, what's more, that in a bullish marketplace many of those tickets went for at least four times their face value. That said, I should mention that I had no set tariff and my asking price may have fluctuated according to whether or not the buyer was a girl I was trying to get in with. On that point, it was extremely noticeable to me how carrying a small wad of Beatles tickets in your back pocket increased your popularity while you were, say, hob-nobbing around the table-tennis table at the youth club, or standing around with a Coke during a dance at the local hall. My social cachet went up exponentially in this period. I had never been quite so much in demand.

I kept four tickets back for myself and three friends, and on the afternoon of New Year's Eve, in a state of high excitement, we took the train up to London from Redhill and travelled on the tube to Finsbury Park. Thrillingly, we were in the street outside the Astoria long before the doors opened and early enough to see the Beatles arrive. I remember a van pulling up, the crowd in the street surging around it in a gale of screaming, some policemen lining up to funnel the band across the pavement, four slight figures ducking and charging for safety. I was close enough to the action to hear John Lennon curse loudly about the manhandling he received – both from the fans trying to tear lumps out of him for souvenirs and the policemen charged with protecting him. The f-word was most certainly used. And then the theatre door slammed and they were gone.

It would be some while before we saw them again. Also on the bill that night: the Barron Knights, Billy J. Kramer & the Dakotas, the Fourmost, the late, great Cilla Black, and Rolf Harris, whom we don't talk about anymore. When they eventually appeared, suited and booted, the Beatles played for a sum total of 25 minutes. Which, looking back at it, was hardly stretching themselves. 'Leave them wanting more' was presumably the strategy – and it's not necessarily a bad one. It's certainly better than leaving them feeling they've had too much.

Still, I will never forget that set-list: The opener? 'Roll

Over, Beethoven'. Then 'All My Loving', followed by 'This Boy', 'I Wanna Be Your Man', 'She Loves You', 'Til There Was You', 'I Want to Hold Your Hand' and 'Money', before they closed with 'Twist and Shout'. And the reason I will never forget that set-list is that Beatles archivists have carefully researched the history of these shows and stored the information online, where I just looked it up. Personally, I don't remember a single detail about the songs that night. In fact, the chances are I couldn't have told you much about them if you had asked me in the street directly afterwards.

Not my fault: as soon as the Beatles strolled out of the wings, the entire theatre went nuts. Everything that happened thereafter was comprehensively buried in screams – mostly from the female portion of the audience, but not exclusively by any means. Consequently, amid this cataclysmic din, the finer points of the performance were lost, along with the less fine points and all points in between. All that musical dexterity honed over months in the clubs of Hamburg – forget it. Frankly, you might as well have put your head inside an industrial extractor fan for those 25 minutes. 'Roll Over, Beethoven'? They could have played Debussy's *Prélude à l'après-midi d'un faune* and none of us would have been any the wiser.

From which I draw the following extremely important conclusion: if you can remember what the Beatles sounded like in concert in 1963, you weren't there.

Note, though, that there's no sign on that set-list of those two initial singles, 'Love Me Do' and 'Please Please Me', but 'She Loves You' definitely got an outing. I was right:

that early stuff was lightweight. 'She Loves You' was the business.

After the show, with our ears still ringing, we headed down to Trafalgar Square to see in the new year – or, perhaps more accurately, to watch other people seeing in the new year. It was a clear night and chilly, but the fountains were full of revellers in variously advanced states of disrepair. The Beatles at the Astoria followed immediately afterwards by New Year's Eve in Trafalgar Square? We felt we were at the centre of the world. Midnight passed, 1963 became 1964, and we drifted back to Victoria station for the early train home.

That was my first business deal, I guess. But was there anything formative about the transaction? Was it the moment the seeds of a future business strategy were planted? In some ways, it was the opposite. There was clear evidence here of the attractions and advantages of getting involved in the buying and selling of glamorous and hotly desirable items. But those were attractions and advantages that I would very deliberately and consistently ignore for the rest of my entrepreneurial life. On sound grounds. But we'll come on to that, and the rationale behind it, in due course.

Meanwhile, I was on the move again. Not long after I made a killing on the Beatles, my father, still on an upward swing, got a job with Dowty, a big engineering firm 120 miles from Reigate, in Cheltenham. Dowty had a division which made equipment for mining and my father was eventually put in charge of their export division, a job which would take him off on business all over the world.

It would also take him immediately to a house in the posh part of Cheltenham at the top of Harp Hill, on the Battledown estate. How posh was this house? It had two bathrooms, that's how posh it was. We had seriously arrived. In under two decades, my father had gone from having no qualifications and living with his parents in a terraced house with an outside privy in Batley to being a sought-after employee dwelling comfortably in the middle-class haven of Cheltenham. His life was a textbook study in social mobility – and mine along with it. Small wonder that issues around the transformation of opportunity would come to occupy so much of my time and energy in later years.

The one inconvenient thing about our move to Cheltenham was that I was halfway through the sixth form at the time. There was a lot of talk about me staying in Reigate somehow so I could finish my A levels without disruption, but it was eventually decided that I should stick with the family. So I ended up spending my second year of sixth form at Cheltenham Grammar, whose alumni included the composer Gustav Holst and Brian Jones of the Rolling Stones (both before my time, of course, although the latter only just), and where the uniform included mortar boards. Of all the indignities. Do you think any teenage boy wants to wander around in a mortar board? Get on a bus in one? Hardly. You were slipping that thing off your head as soon as you were out of sight of the school gate.

Everyone said that moving mid-A levels would be tricky, and they were right. And not just on account of the fancy headgear. Different schools teach subjects in different orders, of course, so I did some things twice and some things not at all, and confusion reigned. Also, the physics teacher hated me. That was the legendary Coot, whom we heard from at the start of this book, telling me I'd only get to Oxford on the bus. (Coot's verdict on Brian Jones of the Rolling Stones, whom he had taught: 'a strange boy'.)

All in all, when the time came to apply to university, my projected grades in maths, physics and chemistry were three 'C's. Remember, too, that, thanks to the great and scandalous syllabus blunder at Reigate Grammar, I had no O level in the subject that I was proposing to take to degree level. With this slightly under-powered CV, it probably didn't surprise anyone when I managed to raise just one generous offer of a place on a chemistry course, from Keele University.

Now, in an ideal world – or even just a slightly smarter one – nobody would apply to university until they had taken their A levels and received their results. That's clearly the logical order in which to do this. It's not just my own experience that leads me to point out how putting applications ahead of results introduces a completely unnecessary layer of hypothesis into the process and is therefore an oddly cumbersome way to go about it. Yet the UK stood firmly by this backward system then and stands firmly by it now, insisting that students apply based on teachers' predictions for their grades and that universities hand out 'offers' in the form of targets which the students do or don't hit. This was an area of the education system upon which, many years later, I would eventually try to put some pressure with the Sutton Trust. We made it our business to find one good reason why exam papers couldn't be marked and university applications completed between June and September. It came down to the fact that university staff don't want to do admissions in the summer, because they have other priorities at that time of the year, such as going on holiday to Tuscany.* Well, everyone needs a break, I guess. But it's a funny way to organize a country's entire tertiary education admissions system.

As it happened, redemption for me arrived in the form of Mr Thomas, the Cheltenham Grammar School chemistry master. Mr Thomas looked strikingly like Claude Rains playing the chief of police, Captain Renault, in *Casablanca* ('Round up the usual suspects!'), so he was known to one and all, though not to his face, as Claude. He was a truly clever man, with a first from Balliol, and, whether because he spotted some kind of potential in me or because he simply pitied me, he took it upon himself to sort me out by giving me extra tuition. He lived at the bottom of Harp Hill, a ten-minute walk from us, and his house had a little room at the back where he and I used to sit across a table

---

* I made this point during a radio discussion once and members of the university teaching profession came after me pretty hard afterwards. 'That's an outrageous and deeply unfair allegation,' they said. 'We can't afford Tuscany.' Well, OK. Maybe not Tuscany necessarily. But the general point stands.

while he patiently filled in some of the unhelpfully wide gaps in my understanding. Needless to say, these sessions, voluntarily given, were priceless. There is nothing as efficient as one-on-one tutoring, as every study in this area will confirm. I ended up getting an 'A' in my chemistry A level, which in those days was some seriously hard currency. In addition to that, I got 'B's in my other two subjects, which, again, was a more than respectable harvest back then. So the headmaster said, 'Maybe you should set the Keele offer aside and try for Oxford or Cambridge.'

At Reigate, it was a big occasion if a pupil was put forward for Oxford or Cambridge. At Cheltenham, it was more common, more expected and less of a big deal. So I learned there and then that certain schools, though technically on a level playing field, connect to the Oxbridge network better than others do. I was also in the fortunate position of having parents who could afford to house and support me while I stayed on at school for the extra autumn term to complete the Oxford entrance exam. Mr Thomas, meanwhile, continued to coach me – and in that I was probably most fortunate of all. A lot of people are lucky enough to find that one teacher who makes all the difference to them; that guy was mine. In 2020 I was pleased to be able to set up the Thomas Award in his honour at the school, which is now known as Pate's. The award is for academic potential in an A level student from a free school meals background.

For Mr Thomas's part, I'm sure it gave him some satisfaction to see one of his pupils turn it around and reward his time and faith by getting into Oxford – Corpus Christi College, to be precise. However, I'm not sure what he would have thought about me getting arrested in my first week.

4

ON TRIAL IN OXFORD

'Do you do this sort of thing often?' asked the Dean of Corpus Christi College, Oxford.

To which the honest answer was, no – never before. Whatever else anyone wanted to say about me ending up in police custody in my opening week at university, it was definitely a personal first.

I guess the mistake was going to Ben Fine's party. Actually, no: the mistake was what I did when I got to that party. Ben was a friend from Cheltenham Grammar who had gone up to Oxford at the same time as me and was at Balliol College, where he had decided to throw a party for his birthday – although I should say that what went by the name of 'party' in this case was really just a bunch of blokes jammed into somebody's room drinking. That night at Ben's, a table groaned with gin, vodka and whisky – the carefully hoarded duty-free bounty from recent trips abroad. Nobody had thought to provide any mixers, so the spirits were going out neat. At the relatively tender age of

19, and by no means a seasoned consumer of gin, vodka or whisky, let alone all three during the same session, I found myself, in almost no time at all, completely and utterly legless.

Inevitably my memories of the evening from that point on are somewhat patchy, but what is clear is that I eventually left the gathering, very unsteadily, in the company of a certain Laurence Eaves, a friend I had made at Corpus. Less drunk than me, Laurence nobly took it upon himself to help me stagger home. A layer of urgency was added to this mission by the fact that it was now approaching midnight, when, in accordance with Corpus's draconian curfew rules, the college gates would be locked and left that way until 7 a.m. As a new student in his first week, Laurence was especially anxious to make that curfew – as I would have been, too, I'm sure, had I not been concentrating so hard on other things, such as staying upright. Either way, it wasn't very helpful of me when, part way along Oxford High Street, with the clock ticking, I passed out in a heap on the pavement. At this point, Laurence weighed his options and decided it was each to his own. He ran for it and left me to the mercy of fate.

Fate, in this instance, turned out to be two policemen in a passing patrol car. One of the officers scraped me off the floor and carted me off to St Aldates police station, where I was shut in a cell. That was where I eventually regained consciousness, at about four in the morning. I had a small amount of time to notice the bars across the window before

I copiously vomited all over the floor. This did not endear me to the officer on duty, who was apparently no fan of students, and especially not of legless ones ('You people think you're the cream … Look at you. You're useless'), and who fetched me a bucket and a mop and instructed me to clean up after myself. Eventually, judging me to have sobered up enough, he threw me out.

It was about five in the morning by now. I hung around on the streets for a while, feeling wretched and presumably looking worse. Eventually the college re-opened and I crawled back to my room and into bed.

And now here I was, a couple of days later, summoned to appear before the Dean, Dr Jamieson, because becoming paralytically drunk and ending up in a police cell in your first week was not something the college was especially keen to encourage in 1966, and probably isn't keen to encourage now.

'You'll be telling your parents, of course,' Jamieson said, as I sat sheepishly in front of him.

I nodded soberly. 'Of course, yes, I will,' I replied, thinking to myself, in fact, that the main upside of this embarrassing débâcle was that my parents would never need to know anything about it, and certainly wouldn't be finding out from me.

'No, you'll be telling them now,' Jamieson said.

He picked up the phone on his desk, rang my father there and then and handed me the receiver. The conversation that followed was a cringe-inducing blend of mumbled apologies (mine) and surprised disappointment (my father's), while the Dean of Corpus Christi College, Oxford, looked on sadly. I've had easier chats on the phone with my dad, let's put it that way. At the same time, the call had come out of the blue for him, so his response wasn't as volcanic as I'd feared it would be. He had angrier things to say about it later, when he'd had time to digest the details.

Anyway, the upshot was that I had to appear in court, in front of a judge, with a public gallery – the full circus. It seems amusing now, not to say over the top, but at the time I was terrified. I wore the only suit I owned and was accompanied by Jamieson, who came to testify on my behalf. As we sat awkwardly together in the waiting room, the clerk came around with his list of the day's business, checking people in. Coming to us, he looked Jamieson up and down and asked, 'What are you in for?'

Jamieson was understandably affronted. 'Jamieson!' he barked loudly. 'Dean of Corpus!'

That seemed to put the clerk straight.

When my case was eventually called, the court heard the testimony of one of the policemen who had picked me up, which he delivered from his notebook in the classic style and which was full of formal, starchy stuff about 'proceeding in an easterly direction along Oxford High Street' and noticing 'the defendant' lying on the ground surrounded by a small group of 'concerned onlookers' (but not Laurence Eaves, clearly). The policeman managed to get a light laugh from the court room by relating how, when he bent down to examine the defendant on the pavement, he could tell

from the overwhelming fumes that rose from the defendant's mouth 'what the problem was'. Jamieson then got up
and vouched for my good character, assuring the judge that
'he comes with the highest recommendations from his
school'. The whole excruciating business probably didn't
take much more than a few minutes, but it felt like a week
before the judge abruptly issued his verdict: 'Drunk and
incapable. Fined £2.'

Now, £2 in 1966 would be the equivalent of about £40
in 2020, so, from a student's point of view, that hurt a bit.
But otherwise this was a result. 'Drunk and incapable' was
not a criminal charge, whereas 'drunk and disorderly'
would have landed me with a criminal record. I was free to
return to college and start living down the shame.

Which, as it happened, turned out to be a rather easy
thing to do. In fact, the main legacy of this episode seemed
to be something far more glamorous: notoriety. The story
of my brush with the law got out, and grew. I didn't need
to do anything: exciting twists were added to the plot quite
independently. 'Lampl's only been up a week and he's
already punching policemen.' I'm not sure I could have
spun it better had I employed a PR team. Suddenly, without
looking for it, I seemed to have gained a reputation as a
rebel. Not so much 'rebel without a cause'; more 'rebel
without a stomach for neat whisky'. But still a rebel.

Anyway, eventually I had to stop basking in my
reputation for hardcore criminality and get on with some
work. My tutor in chemistry at Corpus was Dr Robert
Gasser, which, you would have to say, is a pretty good

name for a chemistry tutor. It was Dr Gasser who had originally interviewed me for a place, grilling me like meat on a barbecue, and every time I went for a tutorial with him, reluctantly wearing the black gown that was obligatory for teaching appointments and lectures, I felt the same nerves that I had felt on interview day. Ordinarily the hour would be devoted to discussing the essay I had just written, although perhaps 'discussing' is the wrong word: 'dissecting' would be better, or maybe 'shredding', and just occasionally 'destroying'. No mercy was shown: the naivety of my young scientific assumptions would be ruthlessly exposed and I would be taken apart in the most brutal manner. Sometimes these would be two-person tutorials, involving me and another student, with Gasser playing us off against each other ('Peter, do you think he's right?') and frequently managing to kill us both simultaneously in the process. Actually, the masochist in me eventually grew to enjoy these sessions. There you were, in a room with the cleverest guy in his area of chemistry, obliged to think on your feet and make a case for yourself or sink. It's quite good for you to have your thinking pulled to pieces every now and again. It teaches you to think again, which turns out is just as important a skill as thinking in the first place.

My college was for men only, and Oxford as a whole was still an overwhelmingly male institution in those days. If you wanted to mix with the opposite sex, you needed to broaden your social circle to include the teacher training colleges and secretarial schools. That aside, socially I felt very comfortable. Yes, there were lots of people around from private schools, but the social mix had entirely changed since the war, and you were more likely to meet someone from a state school than a private one. Laurence Eaves, the friend who was with me (until he bolted) on that night of drunkenness at Balliol, was a Rhondda County Grammar School boy whose father was a bus conductor. His background was far from untypical. Students from grammar schools, as I was, and students who were beneficiaries of the Direct Grant scheme, as many of my friends were, together accounted for approaching two-thirds of the Oxford intake in 1966. In a way that I only fully appreciated much later, we were living through a boom time for educational egalitarianism and social fluidity. It wouldn't last.

In the meantime, though, no wonder I didn't feel out of place. True, there was all this fairy-tale architecture surrounding you the whole time, which could have been intimidating, I suppose, or overwhelming in some way, although, frankly, equally vivid in my memory from those times is the inside of the supermarket where I shopped for pork and pasta, and where, for some reason, the Everly Brothers always seemed to be playing over the Tannoy system. Of course, Oxford was technically my local university, which might have increased my sense of belonging. Cheltenham was only a short hitchhike away, and hitchhiking was a perfectly undaunting thing to do in those days, so I could go home at no expense and have my mother do my laundry, which must have delighted her.

I recall only one real culture clash. There was a girl from St Hilda's whom I was sort of dating, or trying to date. One day she said to me, 'We're going skiing after Christmas, do you want to come?' She said this as naturally as one might say, 'I'm popping to the shops in a minute, do you need anything?' In those days only the very rich went skiing, and certainly not me. I mumbled something about having something else to do. I think that was the end of our dating.

Just as I had at school, I played a lot of sport. Oxford was great for that. I loved the fact that there was this naturally competitive collegiate environment, and, even better, you could just show up and play, which appealed to me far more than devoting time to training. I played tennis and squash and was on the right wing for the legendary Corpus football side that faced Balliol in the Cuppers tournament, where a firmly struck cross somehow ended up bouncing against my knee and flying into the Balliol net – a moment of life-changing glory. I was ecstatic until the referee blew his whistle for offside. Absolute robbery. I was never offside in a million years. If we'd had VAR in those days, the goal would have stood.

Then there was punt racing. You weren't supposed to race punts, you were supposed to steer yourself gently up the River Cherwell, relaxing and absorbing the view in a sedate and orderly manner, but racing was more fun. We'd line up four punts, with two people in each. One of you would punt like crazy for two minutes or so, until you started to feel it, and then you would switch. I used to team up with an Aussie friend called Bob Brandwood, a Teddy

Hall man.* We would set off from Magdalen Bridge and head way upriver, climbing out to push the punt up the metal rollers helpfully placed between different water levels at a couple of places – an extra obstacle on the assault course. At some point we would hit Parson's Pleasure – a secluded piece of parkland set aside for the Oxford nudist crowd. Here, conventionally, women were required to get out of the punt and walk around behind a corrugated fence so they weren't blinded or harmed in other ways by the disgusting sight of unclothed dons sunning themselves. Male punters weren't so lucky.

As for the sport of pot-smoking, which, this being the sixties, was enjoying something of a golden age, I have to report that I tried it (you risked being written off as a gnome† if you didn't), but I never took it up. A mate in my second year was a much better student than I was at the

---

* Life was always interesting around Bob. He later went to work in Paris for Cointreau, the liqueur company, where he earned the unusual distinction of getting fired for sunbathing in the office. Cointreau's premises were on the Champs-Élysées and Bob had a desk by the window where the sun would stream in. This inspired Bob, on one particularly sunny day, to take off his shirt. Max Cointreau, the boss of the company, couldn't believe his eyes when he found somebody soaking up the sun at his desk, and got rid of him. Sometime after that, Bob landed up in Nigeria selling Nivea cream, which some Nigerians thought was an aphrodisiac, so business was pretty hot for a while. For the record, Nivea has no scientifically proven aphrodisiac properties. On the other hand, whatever turns you on.

† A gnome was a square – a conventional, prudish person. Someone who was especially gnomey might earn the term *Gnomenkönig*, from the German, meaning 'king gnome'.

start of the year; three terms of semi-professional weed-consumption later, he was a worse one. Rightly or wrongly, I drew my own conclusions and stuck to alcohol – in far greater moderation than during my first week, I should say. The police were never again involved.

I also discovered that the college's spoil-sport midnight curfew could be defeated. You could (to use the terminology) 'get in over the spikes'. Quite near the gatehouse, two of the iron spikes on top of the tall college wall were slightly askew, making it possible to squeeze through and drop down on the other side. It took a bit of effort, though. Indeed, gate-crashing the college after midnight was its own Olympic discipline. For a start, you needed to maintain a 30-inch waist, which was the maximum you could be carrying if you were going to force yourself between those spikes. Then you needed to be able to get up enough speed to sprint, high-jump, scramble … And very often you needed to be able to do these things while quite drunk, and at serious risk of impalement. (At some point during the manoeuvre, the spikes were at crotch level, which could be unnerving.) Also, in order to have any real chance of completing the mission, you had to start from the other side of the street in order to get up enough speed at the point of launch. Many fell. But if you were lucky, you fell on the college side rather than the road side, and at least then you could take your bruises off to bed.

Eventually you were turfed out of college accommodation and into 'digs', and then you were freer to indulge yourself on your own timetable, of course. Well, slightly freer. In my third year, I was renting a downstairs room in a family house. The rules on entertaining overnight guests were clearly stated, but I ignored them anyway, sneaking a girl down the hallway. Or at least I did until the night my landlord caught me *in flagrante*. It was like a scene from *Sunday Bloody Sunday*. He gave me a full-throttle dressing-down and kicked me out there and then. That meant I was homeless for a short period, before I eventually went to share an apartment with a pal called Martin Bayliss. The house was in Leckford Road and our next-door neighbour was one William Jefferson Clinton, the future 42nd President of the United States of America, but, at the time, a Rhodes Scholar at University College. Not that I knew him. But I found out later that he had lived through the wall at no. 46, and I was able to ask him about it when I met him at an event at the London School of Economics. This was after his presidency, when he went to LSE as a speaker. It was my opening question to him in the five minutes that we had together afterwards: 'How was 46 Leckford Road?' He seemed to remember it fondly and talked with seemingly heartfelt dismay about a new building that had been slung up in the vicinity since then. I didn't mention it that night, but, as I recall, I cooked a lot of tinned sausages and beans in Leckford Road – one of the great student meals. Maybe Bill did the same. Or maybe not.

Meanwhile, challenging sessions with Dr Gasser aside, the pleasures of studying for a degree in chemistry eventually wore thin for me. It was a four-year course, which, looking back, is a lot of specialism for a long time. Not that I regret having done it. Chemistry is a quantitative science, and that's not a bad discipline to acquire. One of the problems with American education is that so few people do science subjects, which partly explains the country's appalling innumeracy levels (40 per cent). Mind you, the UK's figure in that area (30 per cent) isn't much better. A bit more chemistry wouldn't hurt in either of those places.*

But the fourth and final year of my degree course had to be dedicated to a research project. My chosen subject was 'Mechanisms of catalysis on metal surfaces under ultra-high vacuum conditions'. Which is quite a mouthful, and also arguably one of the lousiest chat-up lines ever. The assumption was, if you were academic enough and showed an interest in and aptitude for research, you would go on to do a PhD. But I qualified on none of those counts. I knew this was not how I wanted to spend my life.

But how did I want to spend it? Those years at Oxford were indirectly my first proper introduction to the real world of work. Most vacations I would be looking to make some extra money to supplement my grant. I must have had 15 or 16 really crummy jobs in that period, and I'm sure they all taught me something extremely valuable which I carried with me through life, although in several of

---

* On illiteracy, the US and the UK rank around the same – 20 per cent. In the OECD league tables of 30 advanced countries, these numbers put those countries bottom and second from bottom respectively. That's shocking. Actually, it's a disgrace.

those cases I would have been struggling to put my finger on it at the time.

For instance, I spent a couple of weeks cleaning Oxford's Cowley car works. That was plain grim. These days we think of car factories as bright, spotless places where workers in pristine overalls collaborate with shiny robots on surfaces you could eat your lunch off. This one was a symphony in grease and oil. As a cleaner, the shortest straw you could be given was scrubbing thick globs of car paint off the floors and walls of the paint shop, but other gloomy experiences were available. One day the foreman, a no-nonsense East Ender, dispatched about 50 of us into the workshop's rafters to clean them down as best we could. One guy plaintively called down, 'It's bloody filthy up here! Somebody should have cleaned up before they sent us up.'

Then there was my spell working in a Cheltenham car wash. The other guys used to spray me all the time because I was at Oxford, and therefore posh. Maybe I should have tried quoting those statistics about the university's state school/private school social mix. But they probably would have sprayed me even harder.

At Christmas, I signed up with the Royal Mail at the Cheltenham depot to help sort the Christmas post. Nobody would have got their cards in those days if it hadn't been for the massive seasonal draft of student labour.

In the summer, I picked fruit. The big picking action was in the Vale of Evesham, half an hour north of Cheltenham, and it was here that I proudly picked the blackcurrants that were used to make Ribena. Or, at least, for a short while I did. The thing was, you got paid by weight and I noticed that the girls were earning at least 40 per cent more than the boys at the end of the day. They just seemed to be so much better at it. So I went over to apple picking, which, in a time of rigid workplace divisions according to sex, the girls weren't allowed to do. Apple-picking was more reckless than blackcurrant picking: you were told to just sling a ladder up against the tree and go for it. The dangers of over-reach were ever-present. Also, when you've been standing with the soles of your feet pressed down on the rungs of a ladder all day, your feet don't easily let you forget it. After eight hours in the orchard, you would go home and your soles would spend the rest of the evening trying to convince you that you were still up a ladder.

The one really great gig was at Cheltenham racecourse. Here there was proper fun to be had. You showed up in the morning and would most likely spend the time before lunch clearing up after the previous day's meeting – which in practical terms frequently seemed to mean sitting around and drinking coffee in a greasy spoon.

In the afternoon, when the races took place, you would be given the job of 'treading-in'. You were issued with a large pair of Wellington boots and posted beside a fence somewhere around the course. After the horses had been over and churned up the turf where they landed, you would run out and stamp the ground down ready for the next circuit. The best spot by far was on the last fence – and I quickly got to know the ropes so I could swing that spot for myself every time. From here, unlike with the fences further out, you were in the perfect position, notwithstanding the Wellingtons, to scarper over to the betting ring between races and get a bet on – almost certainly smashing a hole in your eventual earnings, but never mind. Also, from that last fence, you had a decent view of the end of the race. In fact, you had the best view on the course – nearer than any paying customer, right up close, at the very heart of it. To be within touching distance as the jockeys brought the racehorses thundering over the fence, to see horses falling, the jockeys rolling up in a ball, the race powering on around them – you couldn't witness that without being in awe of the bravery and the sheer power of it all. And to get paid for being there? You know, there's a lot to be said for making a fortune in leveraged buy-outs. But this may have been the best job I ever had.

It was certainly better than the few weeks of night-shift I did in a factory that made rubber seals. Life there was pretty slow. Even to my inexperienced eyes, it was readily apparent that there were some major inefficiencies in the production process that were keeping the output down and therefore holding the business back. In the earliest sign of where my professional vocation would eventually lie, I took the initiative and put my thoughts about all this down on paper one evening and presented those findings to management the following morning.

And what do you know? To my quiet satisfaction, management immediately implemented my proposals at shop-floor level, bringing about an instant uptick in productivity, yielding unprecedented performance in that fiscal quarter and significantly boosting shareholder value.

All right, then: no, they didn't. I mean, seriously? Here was some upstart coming in as a summer temp and suddenly handing in a document declaring his vision for the future of the business. It's a wonder the supervisor didn't dump me head-down in the nearest offcuts skip. Instead, showing admirable restraint in the face of my presumptuousness, he accepted my paper with a weak smile. And shortly afterwards, no doubt, he prioritized it by filing it in the nearest waste-paper basket.

That didn't mean I was wrong about the shortcomings of the business, though. Indeed, I suspect there was nothing that I could tell management about systemic inefficiencies in their workplace that they didn't already know. But why change? This was British industry in the 1960s. It was in the vested interest of everybody working in that factory that you didn't do things too quickly.

Back at university, I landed up with a second-class degree. They didn't split degrees into 2:1s and 2:2s in those days, meaning that seconds were a pretty large area to shoot at. But very few people got firsts, so to leave with a second felt good. I was taking away a few other things, too – and not just the knowledge that gin is always to be diluted. Oxford had made me more sociable, it had given me confidence, and it had taught me how to think and how to argue and debate – life skills which would prove valuable to me. But as for what I now wanted to do, I was entirely unclear. Had you pinned me down and forced an answer out of me, I would probably have said something about 'going into business'. But that didn't mean very much and I really didn't know what I was talking about.

In the meantime, my university days had one more beautiful twist to offer. Using money earned by cleaning/ fruit-picking/seal-making, I had bought my first car – a second-hand Mini which I was proud of and which I would possibly have been even more proud of if it had been even part way reliable. It was blue with a white roof, and the white roof meant it could pass for the much faster and much ritzier Mini Cooper – if you squinted. In fact, the car was an absolute lemon. I had it in my fourth year, when I was living in a student house a little outside the city centre, and I think I spent more time pushing that Mini than I did driving it. As my days at Oxford came to an end, I decided I had to get rid of the thing.

Not long after I had taped a 'For Sale' sign to the back window, a young woman appeared at the door of our house. As she was looking around the car, we fell to chatting and she mentioned that she lived in Reigate. I told her that I had been to school there. 'Really?' she said. That was a coincidence. Her father was the headmaster of Reigate Grammar. Maybe I knew him ...

'What? You mean Clogs?' I nearly said, though I managed to stop myself.

I certainly did know him. T. W. H. Holland (known as 'Clogs', and also as 'Thon', but mostly as 'Clogs') and I had come into contact a number of times, most memorably for me the occasion when he saw fit to bend me over a chair in his office and give me 'the swish'. The offence for which I needed caning? Mercilessly playing up the teachers. There was something of a culture of verbal insubordination at Reigate and I confess that I contributed to it. Nothing major, but in those days it was enough. As a consequence, I can report that he employed a run-up from the other side of the room, did Clogs, just for that extra cane-speed at the point of impact. Two hands on the cane's handle, too. I had red stripes on my skin which hurt for a long time afterwards.

Yet look how the planets had aligned. Karma, don't they call it? Yes, Clogs had acted cruelly by flogging me all those years back, but now I had the chance to flog a member of his family a truly terrible car. Perfect.

Assuming she wanted to buy it, of course. Because, obviously, she would be mad to. As she took a perfunctory tour of the outside of the Mini, I braced myself for the inevitable flat rejection. But what do you know? She wanted it! I happily accepted her money, having agreed to knock a little off the asking price as a token of our Reigate connection. There was a nervous moment, of course, when she got behind the wheel. But for once, the Mini actually started and its unsuspecting new owner drove away in it. Sweet revenge!

The next morning, there was another knock at the door. It was Clogs' daughter again. This time, she was accompanied by a large, muscular man to whom she didn't bother introducing me. Neither of them seemed especially happy. That car I had sold her, she began, as the large, muscular man looked on sternly: it wasn't fit for purpose. In fact, it was a piece of junk thinly disguised as a roadworthy vehicle. It wasn't worth the bald tyres it was uneasily sitting on. She would like her money back.

Sometimes, clearly, a tale doesn't get its dream ending. What could I do? I could hardly argue with her assessment of the car, which was accurate in every detail. I suppose I could have told her it was 'sold as seen'. But that bloke she had with her really was very large and very muscular. I fetched her money and, with a shrug and an attempt at a smile, returned it to her. She and her bodyguard walked away, leaving me reunited with that awful Mini.

So near and yet so far. I grimly imagined her in due course relaying the tale to Clogs – of how one of his former pupils had tried to sell her a dodgy automobile. And I imagined Clogs shaking his head regretfully and saying, 'I always had that boy down for a wrong 'un.'

5

CONFESSIONS OF A DRUG DEALER

It's 1970 and I'm driving around in a Ford Cortina with a boot full of drugs and a list of needy customers. My life has certainly taken a dark turn since graduation, you'll be assuming – and, well, it's an opinion. I've become a sales rep for the Beecham Group.

In my extra-large briefcase are samples of anti-allergy medications, stomach products and vitamin supplements. Can I interest you in anything? If you're a GP or a hospital consultant practising on my patch, Wiltshire and Gloucestershire, I'll have a damned good go.

The Cortina is spanking new and a company car. This is huge. In 1970 a young man would move mountains for a dating wagon as supreme as a Ford Cortina. I'm fresh out of college and they're going to give me one? Sign me up.

It's a venerable British institution that I'm working for – and a venerable trade that I'm working in. Why, the Beecham Group's founder himself, Thomas Beecham, started out pedalling home-made laxatives around

Lancashire back in Victorian times. Those laxatives got things moving in any number of senses, and he was soon commissioning his first factory.

The Beecham name would eventually be ploughed below the line by a couple of big mergers and mostly survives nowadays on boxes of over-the-counter flu remedies. In 1970, though, the Beecham Group was a pharmaceutical giant in the UK. Mind you, that didn't mean that all you had to do was drop the name 'Beecham' on the surgery receptionist and 'The doctor will see you now'. On the contrary, the doctor will only see you when he's got through his long list of patients and any other business – and only then if you've successfully charmed the receptionist into letting him know you're there. You're a sales rep, therefore you're a pariah and a nuisance, no matter who you work for.

One afternoon, while I'm sitting with my bulging brief-case in the waiting room of a surgery in Chipping Campden, first in line, an elderly lady arrives.

'Are you a commercial traveller?' she enquires, holding the words 'commercial' and 'traveller' slightly disgustedly, as if with a pair of invisible tweezers.

'Well, I'm a medical rep,' I say.

'Do you mind if I go in front of you?'

Are you serious? When I was here before you, and I've already been sitting here for ages, and I've got a list of appointments that I'm never going to fulfil at this rate?

Although, of course, if I say so, she'll only go and bad-mouth me to the doctor …

'Not at all, madam. You go ahead.'

Today's students will wail aloud to hear it, but if, in 1970, after completing your state-funded university course, you had an Oxford chemistry degree, you were immediately in demand in the workplace. In those days only 7 per cent of the cohort had a university degree; you were a scarce resource. (Now it's 51 per cent.) So, shortly after graduating, I had collected job offers from ICI, BP, Unilever and a couple of other places. And then, in a manner which, looking back, seems cavalier, to put it mildly, without committing to any of them, I had taken myself off backpacking in Greece. By the time I returned, several of those places had been filled. A place at Beecham's came up, though. So Beecham's it was.

The Beecham's job was in marketing – and specifically in 'brand management', which was the hot ticket at that time. It was new and fresh, and everyone was after getting involved in it, and I suppose I kind of went with the flow. But the first thing Beecham's made you do was work in sales – a smart policy, I think. It puts you straight on the front line. If you want to understand a business – its product, its customers – try and sell what it makes.

Before I could be let loose on doctors, though, I had to attend a six-week training course in the Beecham building, a thick-set 11-storey tower on the Great West Road in Brentford, where the red and yellow company flag flew proudly from a mast on the roof. The first three weeks of the course were spent learning about the products, and the second three weeks were spent learning how to sell them. It stood to reason that you would need a firm grasp of the product range. If you're going to flog drugs to doctors, you'd better know what you're talking about.

'So, what did you say this one did?'

'Er, let me just have a look at the box …'

That wasn't going to cut it.

But, Lord, those drug names … You had to know your Floxapen from your Havrix, your Paxil from your Orbenin, your Bactroban from your Reliflex. It was like trying to pick your way through the cast of an Asterix story.

I was coached in product presentation and given video training – filmed in mocked-up action. You saw yourself on a screen – what you looked like and sounded like – and you had your performances picked apart in front of everybody else by the course leader. It was excruciating, of course. But it taught you what worked.

And then, finally, it was out into the field, where a few harsh truths had to be absorbed quite fast. Like the fact that, as a sales rep, you were about as welcome as a gas leak. For the most part, you got treated like a spent piece of gum, which I would say was actually pretty good for you (at least in the short term, early on). Put it this way, it forced you back on yourself and made you try a bit harder. The best chance you could give yourself was to pile into the surgery as early in the morning as you could bear to get there, before the patients started turning up – preferably 8.15 for a surgery starting at 9.00. Then you might find a doctor with three undistracted minutes to give you. Any good grace you had to earn with your own charm and guile – and also with the charm and guile of your free samples. Assuming you could get in to see him, the doctor's first question would invariably be: 'What free samples do you have?' It was good for an Oxford graduate like me to be treated like dross day in, day out.

In the course of these interactions, travelling high and low across Wiltshire and Gloucestershire, I worked out that GPs knew a little about a lot. That's the nature of the job, and if you, as a salesman, knew a lot about your product, you could be talking to them from a position of strength and confidence. The specialists in the hospitals, however, inevitably knew far more than you ever would about their area. So that was the far tougher battleground. (Top tip: See a specialist if ever you can, rather than a GP.)

For my first few days, learning the ropes, I rode shotgun with an outstanding salesman. This guy really knew what he was doing. He may have been the best salesman Beecham's had. He was incredibly low-key. With the best salespeople, you don't even notice they're selling. My appointed mentor would just seem to be chatting, merely passing the time of day. I'd come out afterwards thinking, 'Why didn't he bother to sell anything?' And then I would discover later that the doctor had prescribed a whole stack of product.

The way to learn whether your pitch was getting through, by the way, was to visit the local chemist some time afterwards and find out who was prescribing what. I can still remember the elation of discovering for the first time that a doctor had started prescribing something that I, personally, had talked him into. It felt like a triumph.

Once you had been knocking around for a while, you got to know some of the reps from other drug companies. A sense of mutual respect and sympathy would override the inter-firm rivalry and before long you would be spotting each other on the road, slamming on the brakes, pulling over and flinging open your boots to trade free samples. I realized then that I liked salespeople – and I would grow to like them even more much later. Salespeople are motivated by two things: greed and fear. Say what you like, but there's a lot of clarity in that. Contrary to the stereotype, it makes salespeople refreshingly straightforward to deal with.

Altogether those months on the road were a fantastic experience. I would say now that this may be the best way to prepare yourself for a job in business: go out and be a salesperson. Really, as a primer in the basics – indeed, as an all-round business education – there is nothing to beat it. It will make you a stronger person straight away. When you're selling things, nine times out of ten you're going to fail. Ninety per cent of the time, the person isn't going to be buying. This is a simple fact of life. So you had better learn not to take it personally. Salespeople very quickly acquire the ability to shrug their shoulders in the face of rejection. No dwelling on it: on to the next thing. It's a version of resisting adversity, and it's a precious trait to be able to take with you into the world – business or elsewhere.

Also, when you're a salesperson, you're not high up in some office somewhere, sketching wonderful plans on pieces of paper; you're as close to the guts of a business as you can get, down on the ground, reading the eyes of your customers, measuring the true value of it all. Sales level is where it all gets real. It doesn't matter what you do in life, selling your product, and particularly yourself, is vitally important.

In due course, though, my roaming days as a Beecham's rep were over and it was time to move on to marketing. The end of my stint was announced to me after a sales meeting in Bristol.

'Where are your car keys?' asked my supervisor.

I removed them from my pocket and, without ceremony, he took them from me. That was it. The Ford Cortina was going back. I could have wept.

I managed to say, 'How am I going to get home?'

My supervisor shrugged. 'Try the train?'

After that, I was back in the Brentford headquarters, commuting in from a house I rented with a couple of other guys in Ham, and learning about sales promotions. This didn't seem to make me happy. Coming from a physical chemistry background – quantitative, strictly evidence-based – I found a lot of the stuff I was hearing about the alleged science of marketing quite airy-fairy and suppositious. 'You're saying that if we do A, then B will automatically happen? But why? Where are your tests for that?' I began to think this area might not be for me.

Something else had got into my head, too. In the summer, when I had been at Beecham's for the best part of a year, I had gone backpacking in Greece again and ended up on an island ferry. As usual, the boat was utterly teeming with backpackers, who seemed to be stacked four deep in the sunshine on the upper decks, many of them clutching the acoustic guitars that were practically obligatory for young people travelling in Greece at that time. Squeezing myself into a couple of free square inches, I found myself next to a British guy and practically forced into conversation with him by our proximity. His name was Peter Curtis and he, like me, was not long out of university and newly making his way. Inevitably the conversation came around to the subject of salaries.

'What are you earning?' Peter asked.

My salary at Beecham's was a handsome £1,600, and I proudly told him so.

'What about you?' I said.

Peter told me that he'd just finished at the London Business School and was now starting a job with Monsanto* that was paying him £4,500 a year.

I might have been hot, uncomfortable and surrounded by people with acoustic guitars, but my brain was still working. I thought: 'Wow. That's a hell of a salary.'

---

* The Monsanto Company was among the top American chemical giants and later specialized in biotechnology. It was acquired by Bayer in 2016 for $66 billion.

As soon as I got back to England, I got hold of the requisite forms and applied to the London Business School. If it could work its salary-boosting magic for Peter, maybe it could work its salary-boosting magic for me.

6

GETTING DOWN TO BUSINESS

When I turned up, in 1971, the London Business School had only been in existence for a decade. Yet there was already something established about the place – and not just the beautiful white John Nash building that stretched like some kind of nineteenth-century wedding cake along Sussex Place beside Regent's Park. Unlike the Harvard Business School (up and running since 1908), the LBS was staffed predominantly by scholars – professors and doctors of economics rather than practising or former business leaders. So the school had an academic atmosphere, rather than a vocational one. You were there, you immediately felt, to furrow your brow.

And furrow my brow I did, at lectures on macro-economics and cost-accounting and probability and organizational behaviour, and on a specialist course on decision theory, where the teachers lobbed phrases around like 'stochastic transitivity', 'expected utility' and 'quasi-hyperbolic discounting'. Then there were the parts of the course devoted to case studies, in which someone would present a paper about, say, problems at American Motors, and you would analyse it together. These sessions were rooted in the real world of business and they generally devolved into heated discussions. I think it's fair to say I enjoyed the case studies more than I enjoyed the lectures.

But, overall, the teacher I took most from in those two years in London was Dr Andrew Ehrenberg. He was a German whose parents had fled to England in 1938, like my grandparents, and he had become a leading mind on statistical methodology. The London Business School had made him its Chair of Marketing and Communication just the year before I arrived. He was in his mid-forties, quite wiry and intense, and he had a great way, as a teacher, of listening attentively while you put your theories to him, nodding thoughtfully as he heard you out, and then saying, 'Interesting ... but *wrong*!' There was a lot of clarity and certainty about Ehrenberg – there were things that were right and there were definitely things that were *wrong*! – and he brought that clarity to the course he taught on 'Data Reduction', a subject on which he published a book which I still keep on the shelf in my office. It's about how you take a jumble of figures and distil them down to their essence – the ways you use the numbers you have assembled to tell the story you need to tell. This is an enormously valuable skill, and it turns out that very few people have it, or work on developing it – as anyone will confirm who has ever sat in a meeting staring up blankly at a slide teeming with figures and wondered what they should be looking at, let alone thinking about. With more and more data flying around, this ability seems even more important these days than it did then. One of the key reasons I have been successful with the Sutton Company and the Sutton Trust is that I know how to take a bunch of data from our research and reporting and boil it down to something that speaks to people, and I owe that to Ehrenberg. It was the most important course I ever took.

Another feature of the LBS course was that you were supposed to immerse yourself in a business-related project during the summer break at the end of your first year. This was a work-experience scheme, and I teamed up with my pal David Hall, someone with whom I seemed to be living an eerily parallel life: we were born on the same day, we arrived at the LBS on the same day and we would later join the Boston Consulting Group on the same day. We also shared a passing interest in cars, so for our summer project we approached the Lex Service Group, which had the franchise to import Volvos into the UK. We applied to them to look at ways of potentially expanding their business into trucks. We were handsomely paid for this study, but more importantly, when we showed them the work we had done, which mostly concerned the viability of importing trucks into Britain, they seemed to like it. So we suggested to Lex that we continued our relationship beyond the summer and offered, for a fee, our consultancy services on a part-time basis when school resumed. Lex agreed, and the next term David and I found a small office out of the way at the LBS that nobody seemed to have any use for and covertly turned it into the headquarters of our part-time consulting agency. Here we analysed the pros and cons of getting involved in importing various foreign car brands, presented our findings to Lex and happily banked the fee. I'm not sure whether the powers that be at the LBS would have frowned on this or applauded it, but we kept it under wraps, so the issue never arose. It was a nice little number for our second year – and also something to mention later, when applying for jobs.

Those years at the LBS were altogether a good deal. The school's intake back then was small: 100 students in each of the two years, unlike now, when the school admits nearly 500 MBA students per year. So it was a fairly cosy community. As at Oxford, the population was overwhelmingly male, but that was slowly changing. The year I arrived, women had just made up 3 per cent of the intake for the first time.*

A key detail about the LBS, though (and here again, contemporary students may want to cover their ears): in those days, tuition was free for everyone, and you could apply to the state for a means-tested grant to cover your living expenses for the whole of your two years, which is what I did. For the princely sum of just £4 per week, I had a room in that Nash building in one of London's most desirable residential areas, overlooking the park. I kitted it out with a heavy-duty Bang & Olufsen stereo, from which

* The 2019 intake for the London Business School's MBA class was 40 per cent women. That year's cohort numbered 485.

I would blast out Simon & Garfunkel records and also, when the mood was right, Beethoven's symphonies, of which I was now the proud owner of a box set.

Outside, Regent's Park was essentially our back garden. We could go running around the Inner Circle in the park and kick a ball about on the grass. There were five-a-side football games and students also had access to the squash courts not far away at Lord's. London and all its diversions were spread out before us, but, with the exception of trips to the pubs a short walk away on Baker Street, we rarely felt the need to stray far, even though I had a car in which to do so. (I had replaced the Ford Cortina with a Hillman Minx. Which was less sexy, to say the least. Actually, it was a boxy, family car and by no means what you would have called a single man's passion-wagon. But I got it at a spectacularly good knock-down price from an Italian body-shop guy my parents knew, so I could hardly complain. And, in any case, for two years it mostly languished gathering leaves in the London Business School car park.)

It was at the LBS that I began to think politically for the first time. The hot topic at that point was Britain's membership of what was then the European Economic Community – so nothing much changes, clearly. Britain had applied to join twice in the sixties, only to be vetoed by Charles de Gaulle saying, '*Non!*' But people in the UK, including some of those around me at the business school, were still divided about whether it was a good idea or not. Given my background, it's perhaps unsurprising that I was strongly in favour of EEC membership – and not just for the very sound economic reasons, but for cultural reasons, too. I felt European, and I thought Britain should be European too. Moreover, I felt the London Business School should be a European Business School. (Nowadays it's a fully international school, but that was still a long way off.) I felt heated enough about this theme to set up an informal society at the school, which I titled the European Study Group, and to organize a couple of evening sessions where I invited some experts in to talk about the virtues of being a member of the European Economic Community and the further virtues of the London Business School becoming a fully European institution.

I didn't think there was anything controversial about the group, so I was mystified one morning when Professor Ken Simmonds, Professor of Marketing and International Business, summoned me to his office. A Kiwi who favoured tweed jackets, Simmonds was the London Business School's biggest cheese and a celebrity in business studies circles. Being asked to go and see him evoked eerie memories of being called before the Dean at Corpus Christi, or even of being summoned by Clogs at Reigate Grammar, though I'm fairly sure flogging was off the menu in Simmonds' office. Then again, you could never be sure. Certainly the stakes felt high when I anxiously reported to his room.

It turned out that he was sounding me out about the European Study Group and perhaps trying to work out if I was plotting a coup. At one point in our conversation, he asked, 'Have you always been a rebel?'

I thought, 'Really? This is rebellious? Also, I'm only 24 – what do you mean by "always"?'

Anyway, Britain joined the EEC in January 1973 and confirmed its membership with a referendum in 1975, so job done. The madness of the 2016 vote was a long way distant.

Away from the political frontline, thanks to my covert dealings with the Lex Service Group, I had enough money in the winter of my second year to go skiing for the first time. That girl who stunned me with the offer of a holiday on the slopes back at St Hilda's in Oxford would have been proud of me.

That said, I might have had enough money to go, but that didn't mean I had enough money not to be anxious once I arrived. The chosen destination was Kitzbühel in Austria, and I was accompanied by an old friend from Oxford. One day, after a respectable dinner in a restaurant in Kitzbühel's distinguished medieval town centre, the two of us examined the bill with a sinking heart. The price of everything in these ski resorts was wince-inducing.

There was a long and thoughtful silence.

'We could always do a runner,' suggested my friend.

Naturally I was shocked and appalled that he would even suggest such a thing. Then I read the total on the bill again. And actually he had a point.

We put our heads together and discussed tactics. Too obvious, clearly, for both of us to leave the restaurant at the same time. That way we'd only draw attention to ourselves. Far better if I left on my own while the other guy went to the bathroom. Then he could eventually emerge from the bathroom, quietly leave the restaurant himself and meet me in the street.

So that's what we did. I left in as casual a manner as I could muster and waited outside until my partner in crime appeared. And then the pair of us set off up the street at a sprint. We rounded several corners without looking back and must have put at least half a mile between ourselves and the scene of the crime before we stopped, breathless and laughing our heads off at our own sheer audacity – and at the fact that we were many schillings better off than we might otherwise have been.

At that exact moment, I felt a tap on my shoulder and a voice behind me said evenly, '*Sie haben nicht bezahlt.*'* It was the waiter, who had clearly come hotfoot behind us the whole way. Most galling of all, he didn't even seem to have broken sweat.

We sheepishly walked back to the restaurant with him to settle the bill. We were pleased there were no repercussions. I don't think either of us would have been happy to see the police involved.

After two busy and happy years, I left the London Business School clutching my master's degree. There weren't too many MBAs around in those days, so you felt you were in a select group. And the qualification worked the very specific piece of magic that I was hoping it would: I went into the LBS from a job in marketing that was

* 'You haven't paid.'

paying £1,600 a year and I left for a job in management consultancy that was paying £8,000.* That was a decent return.

That job was with the Boston Consulting Group. In 1973 management consultancy was the shiny new thing, and that's where I saw myself, so I applied to BCG and to McKinsey & Company, who were the two big players in this emergent area. The McKinsey interview process was quite something. It seemed to have a military aspect to it, as though you were applying to Sandhurst or somewhere. The head of recruitment was called Colonel Ambidge. The colonel ran a rule over you, and then, assuming he found you potentially fit for service, dispatched you to Tavistock Square in Bloomsbury for a set of tests under the supervision of a psychiatrist. That was an alarming prospect, although all that actually happened was that you sat some written papers while the psychiatrist paced around the room, occasionally materializing at your shoulder, peering down at your paper and saying things like, 'Hmm, you're really not doing very well on this one, are you?' I think the idea was to get under your skin and provoke a reaction. And fair enough: the point was that consultancy could be stressful. The successful candidate was going to be spending a lot of time working on clients' premises – or in enemy territory, as Colonel Ambidge might have thought of it. That's very different from being

---

* That would be roughly £49,000 in 2019 – a good salary for a post-graduate starting position.

in your own office, surrounded by your own people. And sometimes, if they're doing the job right, a consultant is obliged to operate in a way that is directly antagonistic, and is going to be telling people things about their businesses that they really don't want to hear. So, they would be coming under fire from time to time and, yes, I guess there was a point to seeing how people performed under pressure while a hostile psychiatrist was trying to put them off by giving them some needle. Mind you, those tests seemed to drag on for hours. I got through without snapping, although some other candidates evidently fell by the wayside at that stage.

The Boston Consulting Group didn't insert this additional layer of psychological profiling into their recruitment process. They just talked to you. It was one of a number of ways in which the company felt less structured, less formal, than McKinsey. BCG was new and emerging and entrepreneurial, and the general spirit there definitely appealed to me more. Both companies wanted me to work in their London offices, but I told them both I wanted to go elsewhere. Not that I didn't like London; I just fancied going somewhere new. With both companies, when I mentioned that I was fluent in German, I could practically see a glint enter the interviewer's eyes. Everyone at that time was desperate to start doing consultancy in Germany, but without people who could speak the language, they were stymied. Business always comes down to relationships, and if you're trying to cultivate those relationships across a language gap, it's going to be trickier. Having native-level German in my locker was the clincher for me here – and would prove an enormous advantage to me later on in my career.

McKinsey offered me a job in Düsseldorf; BCG offered me a job in Boston. No disrespect to Düsseldorf, which recently made it to number six in a survey of the world's most liveable cities, but it's not the most exciting place, and it certainly wasn't in 1973. I chose Boston.

So I was off to America – a country where I had never set foot and which mostly existed in my mind in the form of images and phrases collected from TV shows, movies and pop music. It couldn't really be like that, could it?

To help get my bearings, I decided to go from London to Boston the long way – via California. I did this in the company of an American friend from the London Business School, Chris Golis, who had relatives in the country and basically sorted out the whole trip. When we landed in LA, Chris rang his sister, who urged us to head straight down to San Diego to join her for a July 4th beach party. That sounded great, so we told her we would hop on the next Greyhound bus. 'No, no,' said Chris's sister. 'I'll sort you out.' And she magicked up two seats on an internal flight with the airline she worked for – PSA. Boarding the plane for the short hop south, Chris and I were greeted by air hostesses in vanishingly small orange hot pants – the official PSA flight attendant uniform at this particular unreconstructed moment in the history of our culture, although I'm pretty sure British Airways never went that way, even in the seventies.

Next thing I was eating hog roast and drinking cold bottles of beer at a party on Mission Beach, surrounded by impossibly gorgeous women in bikinis who seemed to find my English accent surprisingly interesting. Meanwhile 'California Girls' by the Beach Boys was playing in the background.

And it got better. A few days later, at a Hertz sales lot for ex-rental cars, I got a sweet deal from the woman behind the desk on a bright blue 1972 Ford Mustang. Pausing only to play tennis on California's surprisingly high number of free tennis courts, Chris and I drove that Mustang up the Pacific Coast Highway to San Francisco, where another relative of his, a Berkeley professor, let us stay for a while in his nice house overlooking the bay. From San Francisco we drove back down to San Diego because ... well, because we could, and also because we fancied some more time on the beach down there. And then we drove east across Utah to the astonishing Grand Canyon, and on from there to Las Vegas, which was practically a cow town in those days – a raw gambling place. No theme parks and family hotels and residencies by Elton John at that point. We checked into a Motel 6 charging about five bucks a night and drifted around the casinos. Those places were serving all-you-can-eat breakfasts and dinners for 5 cents, just to lure you in, and we thought that was inspired. But gambling and pulling the handles on slot machines weren't really our thing, and once you had filled up on food there wasn't much else, so we moved out after a night and drove to Aspen in the Rockies, music blaring from the car radio all the way.

After that we stayed with still more of Chris's relatives in Pennsylvania, then carried on right out to Provincetown at the tip of Cape Cod. All the way Chris was asking my advice about his girlfriend, Vivienne. 'Should I marry her, or shouldn't I?' My advice was that he should. (He did. They moved to Sydney and got wed. They're still there.)

And then, having spent some time on the beaches of Cape Cod, I finally headed south to Boston, installed myself in a rented apartment in the Back Bay area, bought a suit and got ready to start my new job with BCG. I had travelled 5,000 miles and discovered that, despite my doubts, America was *exactly* like it was in the movies.

I wouldn't return to live in England for 20 years.

7

CASH COWS AND
QUESTION MARKS

The founder of the Boston Consulting Group was Bruce Henderson, a tall man from Nashville with thick-framed glasses and thinning hair. He was approaching 60 when I joined the company in 1973, exactly ten years after its foundation. That made him 20 or 30 years older than most of the people in the office – the very top recent graduates that he had plucked from the Harvard Business School and from Stanford, although, as you quickly realized, not least of all in the weekly Monday morning meetings that he led, nobody in that office could outsmart Bruce.

Based on his appearance, you wouldn't automatically have picked him out as an entrepreneur; Bruce, too, was a Harvard Business School alumnus, but his university degree, from Vanderbilt, was in engineering, and he had something of the demeanour of a NASA scientist about him. He had a dry sense of humour, too. He used to like asking people, apropos of nothing whatsoever, 'How's your spherical geometry?' It didn't matter who you were. I remember him once putting the question to a top German executive from Siemens. 'How's your spherical geometry?' Cue enormous confusion.

None the less, this was a man who had been vice president of the Westinghouse Corporation when he was only 37, and you don't get to rise so quickly to that kind of height without knowing your way around business at least as well as you know your spherical geometry. In due course, at the start of the sixties, a bank, the Boston Company, had invited him to create a consulting division for them. According to legend, everybody had sat around at a meeting trying to think what the unique selling point of this new division ought to be. When Bruce had suggested 'business strategy', everyone else had turned up their noses. What did 'business strategy' even mean? Nobody out there would have a clue what they were on about. To which Bruce allegedly replied, 'That's the beauty of it. We'll define it.'

And define it he did. Bruce was responsible for a whole cluster of analytical tools and strategies which took shape in the Boston Consulting Group and then moved outwards to inform behaviour right across the corporate world. He was, for instance, the man behind the 'experience curve', which essentially says that if a company doubles output, unit costs are reduced by anything between 20 and 30 per cent, and therefore the faster you grow, the more swiftly you reduce your costs.

He was also the inventor of the 'growth-share matrix', by which you would take all the individual businesses within a company, measure their market growth rate and their relative market share and place them in four categories according to their rating: 'Stars', 'Cash Cows', 'Question Marks' and 'Dogs'. 'Stars' had high market growth rate and high market share, indicating that they merited more investment. 'Cash Cows' were the companies with low growth and high share, which should be milked for cash to reinvest. 'Question Marks' had high growth but low share, which meant that clear-minded decisions needed to be taken about investing in them or getting rid of them, depending on their potential to become 'Stars'. 'Dogs' were low in both share and growth and therefore needed liquidating, divesting or repositioning. The idea was to lose the 'Dogs' and get a balanced portfolio across the other three groups. It was a way to look at a company's businesses and work out which strategy was appropriate for each.

These concepts and many others achieved huge traction in the world of consulting, and by extension in business. When Bruce died in 1992, the *Financial Times* acclaimed him for doing 'more to change the way business is done in the United States than any other man in American business history'.

So, imagine the great good fortune of getting to work at BCG when Henderson was at the helm and, moreover, sitting in an office just across the floor from you. I took so much from the three and a half years I was employed by that company – more, probably, in my first six months in Bruce's orbit than I had taken from the whole two-year course at the London Business School. And that's not an insult to the LBS, it's a tribute to the ideas and energy coming out of Bruce Henderson and the people who worked for him.

It was, in the best sense, a reality check. 'Dream big' was anathema to Bruce, along with all the other vague propositions subscribed to by aspirant entrepreneurs. As he memorably wrote, 'Attempting the impossible is not good strategy. It is just a waste of resources.' Better by far to assemble the numbers and take a view from there. That was a profoundly influential mindset for me, which I took with me to the Sutton Company and then the Sutton Trust – the idea that you should adopt as tenaciously as you can a pragmatism based on the closest available reading of the actual circumstances in which you find yourself. Or to put it more simply: read the data.

For all the intellectual stimulation, however, there is no ignoring the fact that BCG was a very Darwinian place back then. In order to make sure he got the best people on board, Henderson was ready to pay 20 or 30 per cent over the average starting salary for grads of Harvard Business School. In exceptional circumstances, he was known to pay as much as 60 per cent over it. That made BCG about the highest-paying employer for someone coming straight out of business school at that time. But Henderson's attitude was: 'Yes, I will pay extra to secure the best, but then I'm going to feel free to whip them if I need to, and if they don't produce, then I'm going to have no compunction about getting rid of them.'

What determined success at BCG was your 'billability' – how many hours of consultancy you could bill to your clients in a week. There were 40 hours of billable time available in a week. If you could bill 30 hours, that was pretty good. If you were only billing 20 hours, you were in trouble. If you got below 20 for a sustained period, you were fired. Every month on the noticeboard they would pin up a graph on which was mapped everybody's billability, so you could see where you were, and you could see where everybody else was. And you could see some people declining in front of your eyes, and when their performance on the graph dropped below 50 per cent, they were gone – told to clear their desks. It was that brutal.

Something else that was Darwinian: you had to find your own work. I learned that one early. I arrived in the office – the single floor with about 150 people on it that BCG occupied in the 41-storey Boston Company Building at One Boston Place – and was greeted by Bess Wilson, Bruce Henderson's formidable PA. Bess was as hard as nails and effectively ran BCG on a day-to-day basis, doing all the crucial spadework. It was Bess, for instance, who did the face-to-face part of the sackings, informing people that they needed to be gone by lunchtime. It was also Bess, incidentally, who ended up getting married to Bruce.

Anyway, I met with Bess on day one and asked, 'Where do I start?'

She looked askance at me. 'You have to find your *own* work,' she said.

The hierarchy was, in descending order: vice-presidents, managers, consultants. The system was that vice-presidents would find consultancy assignments, managers would manage those assignments and consultants, like me, would get in there and do the grunt work. As a consultant, in order to get the work, you had to go round the vice-presidents and managers and make a case for yourself to be given it. Survival of the fittest again.

And because I had come from London and was new around the place, I had a tough time in the jungle. In fact, in addition to being the new boy, I was the first person straight out of a European business school to whom BCG had handed a start in their Boston office. So that meant I had even more to prove, and even more resistance to break down. The London Business School? What was that? Who had even heard of it? Who was this guy? For the first couple of months, I was wandering around and not really getting very far. Fortunately Bruce gave you a short grace period before your figures on the billability chart mattered, or I would have been out of there before I'd even begun.

But once I had found my feet and begun to get into the rhythm of it, I thought it was terrific. I enjoyed the competitiveness. There was nothing underhand about it, the competition was all out in the open, and there was something tremendously straightforward about that. And the work – once I had managed to attract some – was fascinating. I was going into companies, looking at what they did and developing strategy, working in a team reporting directly to the CEOs. It was pretty fundamental stuff, but very few people were doing it, the science was relatively new and you were working at the cutting edge. Plus there was so much variety. I did work for J. I. Case, a construction equipment company which was trying to compete with Caterpillar. Within weeks of arriving at BCG, I was in Racine, Wisconsin, on the shore of Lake Michigan, the home of J. I. Case, eating pizza at the house of the company's chief executive. It was exciting to find yourself with access to people on the top tier. But that was the Bruce Henderson philosophy: you only did consulting for chief executives. You were the top people, and you only worked with the top people. I also did work for Hershey Foods, the chocolate company. I did work for Draper, a company that made looms for cloth. These were wildly different areas of commerce. And in due course, BCG was taken on by Siemens, the largest company in Germany, which instantly became the biggest client in their portfolio. So then I was involved in developing a strategy for the wide range of electronic components that Siemens produced. I was also saying goodbye to any remaining anxieties about my position on the billability graph. Once I had that account in my brief, my billability soared. I had steady employment.

One thing Siemens was involved in was top-of-the-line dental equipment – the chairs, the stands, the general hardware for dental surgeries – and I was tasked with doing a study for that business. It only had a small market share in the US, and I had to try and work out what to do with this business in that territory. This meant going around and talking to dentists about what they looked for in a dental chair. Shades of working as a rep for Beecham's, I guess. And does anyone actually want to spend time in dental surgeries unless they really have to? But I quickly worked out that dentists wanted Siemens equipment the way they wanted Mercedes cars: because they were superior and German. Around that, I evolved a strategy to improve market share. I was getting an insight into a range of different industries and learning a lot.

I was getting around the country, too. Flying around on company business? That was new to me. On my first trip, I got on the plane and automatically turned right. The stewardess took a look at my boarding pass and corrected me: 'You're at the front end.' Really? Apparently BCG flew everyone first class. Fine by me. Did clients want to be billed for first-class airline tickets for consultants doing grunt work? Perhaps not. But that was all part of the mystique, the self-perpetuating game that says: 'If you want the best, you've got to pay for the best.'

But it wasn't *all* work. There was time for fooling around, too. I made a close pal in the office, Fred Nock, and he and I devoted many hours which could have been billable to devising and executing practical jokes. The more elaborate, the better.

Perhaps the most elaborate was the one we pulled off with Alan Minoff and the Club Med account. Alan was a manager, a top Harvard Business School graduate. He was also a recent divorcé and not disinclined to advertise his interest in the opposite sex. Fred and I asked ourselves:

what assignment would a newly single man with Alan's evident enthusiasms truly relish? Our answer: the Club Med account. A company offering singles-only holidays for horny young adults? The perfect brief for Alan.

Did BCG have the Club Med account? Unfortunately not. But we could always pretend it did ...

Alan's vice-president, Bob Leinhart, was conveniently away in Brazil at the time, so, with the girl in charge of the telex machine in league with us, it was no problem to run up a fake urgent communication for Alan from Leinhart, breaking some glorious news: he had met the president of Banque de Suez, who owned Club Med, and he was now talking to him about working with the company. Alan would be Leinhart's choice to handle the work just as soon as it arrived. In the meantime, he was to keep it secret, obviously.

Alan couldn't contain himself. He went straight to Fred with the telex. 'Holy shit, Fred, I've got this! I can't believe it! Club Med! But don't tell anyone because the whole office will want to work on it ...'

It was already going well. To put a bit more fuel under it, I ordered in a package of Club Med brochures. Fred and I opened it up and inserted a fake covering letter. Then we resealed the envelope, stuck a label with Alan's name on the front and had it delivered to his desk.

Alan's joy only increased. He spent a long time poring over this case material and imagining the pleasures of the flesh that would soon await him on assignment in Martinque. Further fake telexes from Bob Leinhart in the following days suggested that it might be a good idea for him to do a bit of preparatory analysis with Fred Nock and Peter Lampl. That, in turn, enabled the three of us to gather for a couple of top-secret case meetings at which Fred and I could stoke Alan's enthusiasm for the project even further.

We kept this whole thing up for nearly two weeks, at which point Bob Leinhart's return was imminent. So then we faked one final telex in which Bob regretfully informed Alan that the president of Banque de Suez had been involved in a plane crash and was tragically lost at sea – and so, therefore, was the Club Med assignment.

Fred and I went to Alan's desk, where he was still absorbing this shocking and painful news. We told him it was all a practical joke but he refused to believe it, so I picked up the envelope in which the Club Med brochures had arrived and peeled back the label to reveal my name underneath Alan's.

Alan slowly twigged. He then very quickly became incandescent, throwing himself at us. 'I'm going to get you fired!'

Such was his rage that we had to hold him down on the office floor, one of us on either shoulder, to prevent him pummelling us. When he had finally calmed down, we took him out for lunch and made it up to him.

Those first two years at BCG swept by. I was surrounded by the brightest business minds out there. I was learning loads about how companies worked and how they could be made to work better. I was earning good money. Life was great.

Based on the extraordinary success of the Siemens work, BCG decided to open an office in Germany. This was news that interested me – except for one small detail: Bruce Henderson's view seemed to be that the best place for this new BCG outpost was Frankfurt. Now no disrespect, but Frankfurt makes Düsseldorf look like Atlantis. Nobody wants to live in Frankfurt.

But we had this new Siemens assignment, and Siemens was based in Munich – and that was a city I absolutely loved. Indeed, I was still warm with memories of the 1972 summer Olympics there – just a great time. I had been a student at the London Business School at that point, but I had spent that summer with my uncle in Munich, seeing as much of the Olympic Games as I could. Most days you could find people selling tickets in Marienplatz, the central square. Two hours before the event was due to start, those tickets would be changing hands for four times their face value. But if you were prepared to stick it out until the last minute, you might get the same seats for half their price, and sometimes the touts would be practically giving them away. Consequently, for next to no money, I had seats for every day of the athletics in the Olympic Stadium – and good seats, too. Of course, if you left it too late, you might end up with no tickets at all. It was a lesson in the way markets work. You've got to gauge carefully when to dig in.

Anyway, even without the Olympics, I knew Munich to be a great place: buzzy, loads to do, filled with handsome buildings, Alps and lakes within easy reach … So I went to see Bruce Henderson to try and persuade him to make Munich the centre of BCG's German operation.

I sat down in Bruce's office and he immediately pulled out a dossier of charts and graphs showing my compound salary growth, my average billability over the past 12 months ... the full breakdown of my current value to the company. At first I couldn't think why he had assembled all that information, but then I realized.

'Bruce, I'm not here to ask for a pay rise.'

He looked very puzzled.

'Then what the hell *are* you here for?'

I raised the topic of BCG's proposed new German office, and in particular its location. I said I didn't think Bruce would be able to get good people to go and work for him in Frankfurt. (I meant me specifically, but I tried to make it sound broader.) In my opinion, I explained, Munich was a far better choice.

Bruce shook his head. 'It's too far out of the way,' he said.

The conversation was closed and I slunk away.

That seemed to be the end of that. But maybe what I said did get into Bruce's head after all, because not all that long after this exchange BCG announced the opening of its German office, and it was in Munich. Eventually, as the Boston office's resident German speaker, I went out there to help establish that office. I would be there for two years.

When I showed up in Munich, one of my first tasks was to give a presentation at a conference for senior German business executives. BCG was new to the country, so the idea was to gather as many of the top people as we could from all over and expose them to our brilliant way of doing things. This was a pretty high-stakes event, all in all, and I was a fairly junior figure to be charged with the presentation duties. But my German was better than anyone else's who was available. David James, for instance, a Brit who initially ran the Munich office, was known, in similar circumstances, to adopt the tactic of pointing at the slides shown on the overhead projector and saying, '*Das*! *Das*!' in a confident tone. Of Bruce Henderson's German, it was always said that Bruce couldn't really speak the language, but that he understood it perfectly. That was a very smooth way to get around the question.

At that point, though, even though I spoke German fluently, I wouldn't have said that I spoke business German. That would come later, with practice. Nevertheless, I had to stand up in front of all these bigwigs and explain how the BCG portfolio approach worked. Now, at the time we had done the portfolio for all these huge chemical companies – Monsanto, Union Carbide, Dow, DuPont – and the examples in the presentation were all drawn from that work. But of course that work was confidential, so all of the case studies I drew upon and put up slides about were anonymous. Afterwards, when I took questions, the executives in the audience came at me hard: 'Who was it that you were talking about at the beginning there?' 'Which company was it in that second example?' 'Could you tell us who you meant when you said …?' They were peppering me with these questions and even taking guesses. 'Presumably it was

Monsanto you were referring to when you said …?' I kept having to stonewall and say, 'I'm afraid I can't tell you.' All this in the absence of properly fluent business German. Not pleasant. I felt badly exposed. But Bess Wilson gave me some kind words of encouragement. 'These things happen' she said, 'You'll be much better soon.'

There would be other struggles. I continued to consult for Siemens, but on the ground now, on their premises. But that work turned into a bit of a battle for a while. At that point Siemens was in the mainframe computer business, but losing 30 per cent on sales. They couldn't compete with IBM who, in those days, had 70 per cent of the global market. Siemens was leasing its computers to clients and the computers were getting returned sooner than predicted because IBM was coming out with new stuff and making them obsolete. I thought Siemens was over-accounting and being unduly optimistic about how long this stuff would stay out. All of our analysis suggested that they would never make money in that business and ought to get out. This was stressful news to deliver. You're in meetings with all the divisional heads and essentially you're saying that one of those divisions doesn't work. You're telling them to their faces. But that was our conclusion, and it was one of those cases where the client didn't want to hear it. So there was a big fight between BCG (and me in particular) and the Siemens guys. They didn't get out because they were so proud – they were one of the highest tech companies in the world. It would have hurt them to back down. So, after a long fight, they turned our advice down.

Still, Munich turned out to be as much fun to live in as I had assumed it would be. Fred Nock had come out to join the Munich office, too. I lived in an apartment in Bogenhausen, which was one of the nicest residential areas, and I was right by Käfer, which was one of the city's best restaurants. I spent my evenings in the wonderful jazz clubs in the Schwabing-Freimann district. I had a BMW 2002 saloon car, which went like a bomb. And there were no speed limits on German autobahns, so it was a very good place to own one. The Alps and the lakes were just a short drive away. In the summer I learned to windsurf on the lakes. Every weekend in the winter I would drive into the mountains and ski. There was a lot to like.

It was while skiing, across the border in Austria, that I met an English girl called Janet Clowes, who was on holiday. Janet was a student at the University of Kent, reading English, and after a few days she went back to Canterbury. But I was smitten with her and invited her out to Munich one weekend. We started seeing each other as regularly as we could across the distance. Eventually she quit her course at the University of Kent and moved to Munich to live with me. After about a year of being together, we decided to get married.

The wedding was on a Saturday at Corpus Christi College in Oxford. I wore a suit and the bride wore pink. My parents came, and my sister. Fred Nock was my best man as I was his in Maine a few years earlier. Laurence Eaves, my old college pal and the man who had abandoned me in my hour of drunken need on Oxford High Street, was there, too. It was the July of 1976, an exceptionally hot summer in the UK, and the college lawn, usually lush green, was baked brown. Nothing else about the place seemed different, though. Late in the evening, when drink had been taken, Laurence challenged me to 'get in over the spikes' – vault the college wall, like in the old days of the midnight curfew.

Crazy suggestion. The run, the leap, the scramble ... Let's face it, that was a student's game. It had been more than eight years. I wasn't a kid any more, I was a grown-up, a management consultant. A married man, indeed. I'd never make it.

I did, though.

8

SEEING THE WOOD
FOR THE TREES

The honeymoon was in Italy, beginning in Venice, then driving down the east coast before crossing over and coming back up the other side, through Pompeii and Naples and on to Rome. Among many other things, it was an opportunity to learn that if you can drive in Naples, where the roads are as narrow as drainpipes, where cars and Vespas and pedestrians hurtle at you from every angle, and where the signs and road-markings are just there as rough suggestions of things that you might like to consider at some point on your journey, well, then you can probably drive anywhere. Other parts of the trip were far more relaxing. We had nothing booked: we just pitched up in places and figured it out from there. I guess the whole marriage was a bit like that: act on impulse, work out the details later. Perhaps that's why it wasn't destined to last very long.

Back in Munich, cracks began to appear pretty quickly. Janet didn't speak any German, and if you don't speak the language of the country you are living in, it's not easy. If you can't even turn on the telly and understand what people are saying, then you can soon start to feel isolated. Making friends is tough, too. I was working long hours and Janet was often alone. She began German lessons, but her unease in Munich continued.

Much as I loved Munich, I was becoming fretful, too. Consultancy is a great place to set out from, but, by definition, it was off to one side of the action. It was *about* business, but it wasn't *actual* business. A consultant, as the saying goes, is someone who knows 21 different ways to make love but doesn't know any women. And by this point I had spent three and a half years doing it. The macho aspiration in those days was to become a general manager – to take charge of something. So, with a view to solving both my own restlessness and Janet's unhappiness, I decided to move back to the States.

Perhaps the simplest thing would have been to stay with the Boston Consulting Group and go back to Boston. However, the fact was that I was extremely valuable to BCG in Germany, where they were continuing to expand. So they had no motive to re-import me. Additionally, I was looking to move from consulting into general management.

BCG alumni were extremely sought-after. BCG had become a major brand, and everybody seemed to want to hire someone from BCG to do their strategy. So I got a few offers quite quickly, all from companies who wanted me to do strategic planning for them. But the most attractive deal on the table was from International Paper, the forest products giant based in New York, which was, in fact, a client of BCG. It was also a Dow 30 company, which was compelling: there was a lot of prestige attached to working for a Dow 30 company. Their proposition was that I would start out doing strategy work and then, if it all panned out, I could move up into general management. The offer met my ambition: the salary was exceptional (I was on $40,000 at BCG and International Paper was offering $70,000); the company was based in the Daily News building, which was on 42nd Street between Second and Third, in midtown Manhattan; and New York altogether felt very attractive – not just to me but also to Janet. On top of that, International Paper agreed to get me a Green Card.

So in 1977 we packed up our things in Munich and left for New York.

The city was still crawling out from under the fiscal crisis it had suffered in the mid-1970s and was practically bankrupt. It was a far darker, dirtier, edgier place than it is now – a place where, even in midtown Manhattan, you were extremely careful where you walked at night. But I loved it. I loved the energy, the outwardness, the spontaneity. I loved the fact that in the morning you wouldn't have any clear idea where you would be having dinner that night. I loved the fact that nobody seemed to be putting things in the diary for a fortnight's time.

I also loved the way that, at that point in the city's history, you could pick up property for knock-down prices. I found a five-room apartment on Beekman Place, by the East River, one of the nicest addresses in New York, for $58,000, which was less than the $70,000 I was earning a year. That was a seriously good deal. Janet got a place at Colombia University to carry on her studies and I went off to work at the Daily News building.

International Paper had come together at the end of the nineteenth century as a small collection of paper and pulp mills on the Hudson River in upstate New York. Now it owned 8.5 million acres – massive landholdings in thousands of parcels, sprayed all across North America, most devoted to growing trees. When I joined, the joint number two at the company was Donald P. Brennan, a business prodigy who had risen to the top of this enormous company by the age of 35. He was a tough, no-nonsense figure, and people in the office by and large stepped rather warily around him. But I always felt that he and I got along well. Eventually he moved on to the investment bank Morgan Stanley, where he was head of private equity, and after that he retired to live variously in a huge mansion in Florida, a lovely place on North Fork, Long Island, and an 1,100-acre farm in Virginia, an hour and a half from Washington, a 17-bedroom estate called Llangollen, whose land included 400 acres of forest and four polo fields and extended away into the Blue Ridge Mountains. He liked to point out that the property had four miles of stacked stone walls around its perimeter and that not one of those stones was out of place. You could say he was a bit of a perfectionist.* But

---

* He was also, I think I'm correct in saying, the only person I had ever met who collected vintage military saddles. At one time he had more than fifty of them, expertly curated, including many that had been sat on during key moments of the American Civil War.

what with the trust he placed in me at International Paper and later in the deals he alerted me to and supported me in while he was at Morgan Stanley and I was trying to go it alone, it's not an exaggeration to state that Donald Brennan was the most influential person in my business life. Without him, I wouldn't have been as successful.

Work went well and I quite quickly got promoted to director of strategic planning for half the company. The set-up was that one half of International Paper was run by Brennan, who was vice-chairman, and the other half was run by a man called Ron Goode, a nice guy from an engineering background, who was also a vice-chairman, and I was working for Goode at this stage.

Our Canadian company, Canadian International Paper, was agitating to bring in a new newsprint mill in the south. It was going to be a huge state-of-the-art affair, costing a fortune. Ron sent me up to Montreal for a couple of days to have a look at the project. I came back to New York and told him that, having gone over the data, I thought it was a disaster. I ran through a bunch of slides, and Ron could see very plainly that this thing was a lemon.

So, there followed a meeting in New York at which I was required to present my findings to an audience including Ron, Donald Brennan, Ed Gee, who was chairman and CEO, Paul O'Neill, vice-president of strategic planning, and the president of Canadian International Paper, Ces Flenniken, who had flown in at the head of the Canadian contingent. Comedians like to say that Glasgow is a tough crowd to please, but this wasn't an easy one either.

I gave my presentation which essentially boiled down to the simple message: 'This plan sucks.' That was not a message the Canadians were pleased to hear. When I had finished, an almighty bun-fight kicked off, with Ces Flenniken hitting back at my dismissal of the project and Paul O'Neill pitching in to defend me. O'Neill, who had been the deputy director of the Office of Management and Budget in the Ford administration, was a straight-talker who took no prisoners verbally. He would later be famous for that trait as George W. Bush's US Treasury Secretary.*

So O'Neill was tearing into Flenniken. And then Donald Brennan launched in and started berating me and O'Neill, asking us what we thought we were doing, pillorying this plan. Clearly angry about the scenes he was witnessing, Brennan brought the meeting to a close by insisting on a ceasefire, the terms being that O'Neill and I would go up to Montreal a little later to discuss this matter further with our Canadian colleagues, ideally in a more civil atmosphere.

I went back to my desk feeling thoroughly reprimanded. I felt no more at ease when the phone rang almost immediately and it was Brennan.

'Come up to my office straight away.'

This didn't seem to augur well.

---

* Paul O'Neill is probably the only US Treasury Secretary ever to have described the US income tax code as '9,500 pages of gibberish'. In 2001 he was accused of a lack of sympathy when his response to the worst week of declines by the Dow-Jones index in 11 years was: 'Markets go up and markets go down.'

But in fact Brennan seemed much more relaxed than he had appeared a few minutes earlier.

'Look,' he said, 'the reason I stepped in is, it just wasn't fair. Ces is a paper-mill guy – you and Paul O'Neill were just beating him up. Now, tell me again what the deal is here, would you?'

I went over my argument again, explaining why I was so sure the company shouldn't go anywhere near this project. Brennan listened without commenting. I left feeling much calmer, but I still wasn't sure that I had 100 per cent convinced him.

After the cooling-off period, Paul O'Neill and I flew up to Montreal for round two. We were still advocating against the deal, but, chastened by the earlier experience in New York, we were ready to be more diplomatic about the way that we did so.

Canadian International Paper's office was in the Sun Life building – a real barn of a building. Indeed, when it had been completed, in the thirties, it had been able to boast of being the largest building in the British Empire. O'Neill and I were shown to a conference room, where we waited for half an hour with a whole bunch of Canadian executives. Then Ces Flenniken came in. Before we could even offer a greeting, he unleashed a torrent of abuse at us, a monologue of insults which must have lasted about 20 minutes and which concluded with the sentences: 'Get out of here. I don't ever want to see you again.'

So much for the cooling-off period. O'Neill and I got a cab back to the airport, where all the flights out to New

York were fully booked, meaning we had to sit around for ages before finally shuffling home late at night. But at least that terrible newsprint-mill venture was off the table.

Then Ron Goode and Donald Brennan switched positions in the company and I ended up working for Brennan. This was when I got to learn more about him – like, for instance, his fondness, from time to time, for driving his Mercedes around Long Island while standing up with his head poking through its sun-roof. I also learned that he had the constitution of an ox. A night out drinking with Brennan on a business trip could wipe out lesser mortals, such as myself, not just for the following day but the one after, too. Little wonder that my colleague Minge Reid had the habit of looking to the heavens and breathing 'Donald P.' in mock worshipful tones at the mention of Brennan's name.

One member of the team who didn't seem overawed was Mark Wray, who was a wise-guy with a deadpan tone of voice. One day he arrived late for a meeting that Brennan was heading. Brennan, not pleased, asked him what had kept him.

'I went to have a haircut,' Mark replied casually.

Everyone else in the room winced. This wasn't really the kind of excuse that you wanted to be offering 'Donald P.'.

'A haircut? On company time?' said Brennan.

'Well, it *grows* on company time,' replied Wray.

Even Brennan had no answer to that.

One Friday afternoon Brennan gave me a stack of paperwork and said, 'This is totally confidential: we're thinking of selling Canadian International Paper.'

This was quite something. Canadian International Paper represented a third of the company, with millions of acres of timberlands in its portfolio. I took the paperwork home and worked through it on the kitchen table all weekend. There were a number of issues in play, but the most serious among them was the possibility that the state of Quebec would become independent of Canada. In 1976, the Parti Québécois, who were separatists, had won control of the provincial government and were promising to put the issue of sovereignty to the people in a referendum. We owned a lot of land in Quebec and there were concerns about the future of that land in the event that separation took place. It was possible that we might even lose it all.

The separation never happened in the end – the people voted against it in 1980, and again, extremely narrowly, in 1995 – but it was a very real threat at this point. Taking everything into consideration, I concluded that we should sell the company and gave that opinion to Brennan on the Monday.

In due course, we were arriving in Toronto to negotiate the potential sale of Canadian International Paper to Canadian Pacific, the largest company in Canada. Naturally, given the magnitude of the deal, the atmosphere in the car taking us from the airport to the Royal York Hotel was tense, with everybody absorbed by the prospect of the monumental business that lay ahead. Or maybe not entirely absorbed. Along the way a guy overtook us on a huge motorbike with a girl riding pillion, her long blonde hair streaming out behind her. Brennan, sitting in the front, turned to those of us in the back, sighed wistfully and said, 'That guy is doing a lot better than I am.'

While this deal was going on, I witnessed what a great negotiator Brennan was. First Boston was the investment bank for International Paper, but Brennan knew that Morgan Stanley was keen to pick up the business. When you do a major deal in a public company, you have to get a 'fairness opinion' to take to the board – an assessment of the fairness of the price, which you commission from an independent bank. Brennan met with Morgan Stanley and said, 'You want our work at some point. Do this fairness opinion for me for $100,000, and then maybe, further down the line, we can talk about the other stuff.' Morgan Stanley, understandably, before committing to anything wanted to know what the deal was that Brennan needed a fairness opinion on. But Brennan wouldn't tell them. He insisted it was confidential at this stage. 'Say you'll do the opinion for $100,000 and then I'll brief you in due course.' So Morgan Stanley signed up – and Brennan got himself a staggeringly cheap fairness opinion. Canadian International Paper was sold to Canadian Pacific for $1.1 billion. At that time it was the biggest deal that had ever been done in the forestry products industry.

I did strategic development for a while. Indeed, it took me a bit longer than I had hoped to make that promised transition into general management. Finally, though, in 1980, Brennan called me into his office. He said, 'You look too young for this, but I'm going to do it anyway.' And then promoted me to president of International Paper Realty and general manager of the land utilization division – which, I have to say, looked pretty good on the business cards. What that title meant was that I was now responsible for the utilization of the land in the company's portfolio, and all of the company's land deals. It was a big job for a 32-year-old.

Now, almost all the land the company owned was given over to growing trees. If you convert this land into real estate, you increase the value of that land enormously. With the land we took out of the company, we did two things: we either sold it or we developed it. From time to time International Paper needed to top up earnings for that particular quarter. Then I would have to sell some land as fast as I could. I had the numbers of some guys I could tap up at short notice to do a deal – good old Southern boys, a lot of them, based down south where it is hot and wet and the trees grow faster than they do in the north. Among them was Billy Belote, a man who seemed to own half of Belize, though I never quite worked out how or why. He was on the north side of 70, charming and addicted to doing timberland deals. I used to call him up: 'Hey, Billy, we need to sell. Can you take it?' And almost invariably he could.

Meanwhile, the pension funds were starting to come into timberland, too, recognizing it as a good, steady, long-term investment. At one point during my tenure, International Paper accounted for 20 per cent of major land transactions in North America. I reckon I knew more about major land deals at that time than anybody in the US.

When it came to developing our land, there were essentially three kinds of project: ski resorts, golf courses and beachfront developments. Golf courses were potentially a sweet deal. You need somewhere between 150 and 200 acres to build a golf course. We would sell that land to a developer for a dollar. He would develop the golf course and then the land around it, which we owned, was worth $50,000 an acre when it had been worth about $500 an acre as timberland.

I'm not pleading hardship when I say that my work as President of International Paper Realty in those days was taking me to golf courses and ski resorts on a regular basis. Purely for research purposes, you understand. I didn't play golf in those days. But I loved skiing, so this was a perk and a half. If you're going on a business trip and you're packing your skis, you know you've chosen the right job.

My boss was John Dillon, another strong Irish-American with whom I rubbed along well, and he really knew how to ski. In an earlier life, he had been a ski patrolman at Lake Placid, and those ski patrol guys ski better than the instructors. We would set off to resorts together on reconnaissance missions. Lessons were learned on these voyages – and not just skiing lessons. International Paper owned land around two ski resorts in Vermont – one in Stratton and one in Killington. The Stratton land had been built out, but at Killington we persuaded the owners of the resort to put in a new ski-lift over our land. All of a sudden, with the resort footing the bill for the lift, we got a pile of land that was worth a fortune. Because just as people like living on golf courses, they also like owning places by ski resorts, especially if those places are luxury condos offering super-convenient ski-in/ski-out facilities. We had enough land to build 2,000 units – a virtual town of high-end condos. Hog heaven. Except in this case, quite rightly, the environmental people shut us down and we ended up building just 200 of them. Still, even those 200 made us a lot of money.

There was always an environmental battle to be waged with these developments, and I'm not proud of one of the fights that my position got me into at that time. Nothing to do with golf or skiing in this case. International Paper owned some wetlands in South Carolina and Georgia. Wetlands aren't worth anything – unless you're a bird, of course, in which case they're worth quite a lot. But if you drain them you can make good agricultural land out of them – and that's worth big money. In order to turn a profit, International Paper got involved in draining some of its South Carolina wetlands to sell them for farmland. This project brought the US government's environmental people running. We were shut down on that development, and quite rightly, but we shouldn't have been gunning for it in the first place, and, looking back, I wish that I'd had no part in it at all rather than followed the company line on it. I can only hold up my hands. Much later, after I had left the company and educated myself a bit more environmentally, I realized what a disgraceful thing this had been, and I went through some guilt about it, to the extent that I named the US environmental organization the Sierra Club and the bird wildlife trust the Audubon Society as beneficiaries in my will.

After Donald Brennan left for Morgan Stanley, I ended up working for John Georges who had been a senior executive for the chemicals company DuPont. Georges heard about the possibility of buying the second largest paper company in Mexico. This was attractive because it would give International Paper a substantial foothold in Central America. We would need to go down and check out the company's holdings and I was assigned to lead the expedition.

In Mexico we chartered a plane to fly our inspection party around for a day of visiting variously remotely located sawmills and paper mills. This would have been a lot more fun if I hadn't chosen the night before to get struck down by the worst case of Montezuma's Revenge that I can recall experiencing. Montezuma's Revenge is a testing condition in any circumstances, but try having it while bumping through the air between sawmills in Mexico. I quickly realized, as the plane lurched on, and as my stomach lurched on with it, that I had two choices: either to jump out without a parachute and take my chances, or to ask the pilot to put the plane back on the ground at the nearest opportunity. Otherwise things were going to become incredibly uncomfortable in that cramped interior – and not just for me, but for the rest of the party, too. I chose the second of those options. The pilot set the plane down on a relatively nearby airstrip, bang in the middle of absolutely nowhere. I got out and lay down on the tarmac.

The plane took off and the touring party went on without me. I closed my eyes, listened to the birds and insects and waited for the waves of nausea to calm. Several hours later, the plane returned to pick me up. So much for leading the expedition. (We didn't buy the company in the end, but that was entirely for strategic reasons and had absolutely nothing to do with my having suffered at the hands of Montezuma during the review process.)

Away from work, I took out another mortgage and bought a one-storey, three-bedroom house on Mauritius Bay on Long Island. Again, I was lucky: the deflation in real estate at the time meant that I picked it up for $100,000. With my salary and bonuses, it was easily within reach. I put in a pool and started driving out there every weekend, hitting the parties and the tennis club, relaxing at a bar called the Red Fox and resuming the windsurfing that I had started in Munich. I could put the board in the water direct from the house and there were races every Sunday.

And from there, it was just a small step to competing in the 1981 North American Windsurfing Championships in Cancun, Mexico. No, seriously. Actually that may not have been quite as big a deal as it sounds. The sport of windsurfing was in its infancy. There was no big qualifying procedure for the championships. If you fancied your chances, you could go down there and sign up. So I did, flying down with Peter Carroll, a friend from the London Business School who was now working for Chase Manhattan Bank. The race course was marked out by buoys on the open sea, and that day the waves were washing through about four feet high. I had learned to surf on lakes and in bays, and it was no real preparation. You simply didn't see big wave-action on the Starnberger See near Munich, or even in Mauritius Bay. Accordingly, when the gun went for my qualifying race, I considered myself lucky to get over the start line. Immediately thereafter, I was wiped out. I scrambled back up on the board, only to be wiped out again. That pretty much set the tone for the next half an hour. I must have crossed the start line at least half a dozen times. I wrestled with the waves and the waves emphatically won. I think about 100 of us set off on that race and fewer than ten of us made it as far as the first buoy. I was not among them.

Ah well. Club Med hosted a competitors' dinner that night, which was decent of them, and we all got pleasantly drunk. And as I recall, the legendary Robby Naish, who was only 13 years old at that point, and who had grown up in Hawaii rather than Wakefield in Yorkshire, swept all before him in the competitions. But that wasn't unusual: he would go on to win the World Championship 23 times. He also staged an unlikely comeback at Maui just a few years ago. Maybe I should do the same.

One thing is for sure: without windsurfing, there would possibly have been no big deal in Seattle, as we saw back at the start of this book. And without that big deal in Seattle, I would probably have gone bankrupt. To that extent, like Robby Naish, I owe it all to windsurfing.

Along the way, Janet and I had drifted apart. She was a student, I was in the business world; our lives didn't match up very successfully and we were struggling to find things in common. We separated very amicably and kept in touch for a long while after. She ended up going to Brazil and marrying again, and later she went to live in San Francisco. Neither of us had any lasting regrets.

Meanwhile, work continued to go well, but having reached the stage where I was running something, I began hankering to run something of my own. I had no real idea how to bring it about, though. Then one day I sold one of International Paper's unwanted businesses to Peter Orthwein, a polo-playing entrepreneur and friend of the extravagant Peter Brant, whom we met during the unfortunate legal case in Chapter 1. It was Orthwein who introduced me to Brant. He was the co-founder of Thor Industries, which was in the recreational vehicles business, but what I was selling him from International Paper's portfolio was an unrelated business making kitchen cabinets. There was nothing remarkable about the deal, really – except that Orthwein wasn't putting up any money of his own. That got my attention. He was acquiring a business using entirely borrowed funds.

Somewhere in my head, a large, bright lightbulb went on.

9

MAKING SOME MONEY

We look back on the eighties as a time of rape and pillage in the world of business – the age of the corporate raider, of rampant aggression and grave acts of cold-blooded, money-led immorality by Wall Street types in red braces and contrast-collar shirts. In which respect, Michael Douglas and that Oliver Stone movie have a lot to answer for. So let me state for the record: I never wore red braces. I might have had some contrast-collar shirts for a while. But red braces? No.

Still, I suppose I was, to some extent, a crusader at the dawn of leveraged buy-outs – the tactic of purchasing companies with debt and a little bit of equity. That stuff became commonplace. But when I entered the fray, it was a relatively new game.

There were some important distinctions, though, between the way my new company, the Sutton Company, went about its business and the general drift. And it might be worth stating up front that I didn't start the Sutton

Company in order to become wealthy. I know that's an easy statement to make when you did, in fact, end up becoming wealthy. But it's true: making a lot of money by the shortest route possible was not the founding vision, as it might have been in certain other acquisitive eighties operations. Yes, if things went OK, I thought I would be comfortably off, just as I had been while working for International Paper. But first and foremost I was looking for the personal satisfaction of running something – and more specifically, running something of my own. That was the initial spark. I always was strongly entrepreneurial by temperament – dating back, you might say, to the days when you could pick up Beatles tickets in clumps – and there is a certain kind of single-mindedness that comes with that mentality that wants to forge its own way. It was worth a lot, I figured, not to have a boss. Even if your boss was a really great person (which was true of nearly all of the bosses I ever had), it was worth a lot not to take orders. The way I saw it, in 1983, after more than a decade of working for others, independence was worth more to me than money.

Another thing to stress: everything the Sutton Company bought, we bought with a view to improving profitability through our own hands-on work. Management was key, and management was how we created value. This wasn't fund-raising. We weren't going around and raising money for something so that we could take our 2 per cent management fee and then, later, our 20 per cent of the upside – the 'two and twenty' fee structure (or cartel, as one might refer to it, given how much 2 per cent is of the vast sums that are raised today). Leveraged buy-outs have morphed into private equity, which amounts to raising money to take the 2 per cent. We were getting hold of companies in order to improve their profitability ourselves – and, consequently, our fee structure was 'zero and 100'. Which is to say, no management fee, but all of the upside.

In fact, my initial idea for the Sutton Company was to stick to land deals. They were what I knew. As I mentioned earlier, at that time pension funds, which take a long view, were beginning to see timberland as an investment. Timberland appreciates in value: it goes up with inflation; the trees grow, and as they grow, they change from pulp wood to saw timber, which is higher value. It's good and steady, and my objective was to get into this newly expanding field and represent those investors – effectively switching to the other side of the table from the one that I had been on when I was running the land utilization at International Paper.

The Boston Company, which had been the parent of the Boston Consulting Group, approached me to put a timberland fund together. The idea was to get several pension companies to pay into the fund and then for me to buy timberland with it on the funders' behalf. For many weeks I worked my socks off, going around pension companies with the Boston Company, explaining why timberland was a good investment and trying to get them to buy into the project. I thought it was really promising and I was gutted when the Boston Company, for reasons I still don't entirely understand, eventually went cold on the idea and pulled the plug. That was my first fresh-air shot in the Sutton Company's early days.

Then there was the unfortunate piece of business involving Peter Brant and the piece of timberland in Virginia, which I wrote about earlier, and which ended up ticking away expensively in a lawyer's office.

In and around these frustrating times, just in order to see some money coming into the company, I resorted to doing a bit of consultancy work on the side. And even that didn't always go entirely to plan. I consulted for a company called Calfat, which sold luxury bedsheets to stores like Bloomingdale's and Macy's. The owners were interested in selling the business and wanted me to act as an intermediary. They were an extremely wealthy Brazilian family based in São Paulo and they flew me down to their home there to discuss things. I seized on this as a unique opportunity to see how the other half lived down in Brazil – which, as it turned out, was behind 20-feet walls and with armed guards accompanying them everywhere to keep potential kidnappers at bay.

The boss was quite the playboy. We were in his house, soberly discussing the future of his business, when he suddenly looked at his watch. 'It's 6 o'clock,' he announced. 'Let's go have some fun.'

Well, I guess it's never too early. We jumped into a car and, with armed guards in close attendance, set off for an active tour of São Paulo's finest high-end samba clubs. The designer of the bedsheets, who was a guy from New York, was with us, and during the evening I became aware that he had taken quite a shine to me. I, meanwhile, seemed to have taken quite a shine to the Brazilian women dancing in the clubs. So the designer was chasing me, and I was chasing the Brazilian girls and, as business trips relating to garment company buy-outs go, I would say the evening passed off rather electrically. But the company never got round to paying me.

After the best part of a year of this kind of fruitless battling, I decided I needed reinforcements. I made the mistake of appointing a guy who had worked with the chief executive at Bloomingdale's, but who seemed to think my company's lack of ongoing business was a perk of the job rather than a dangerous crater in urgent need of filling.

'This job is great,' he said one day, when I walked in and found him with his feet up on the desk. 'You can read the paper all day.'

He was out by the end of the week.

But at least I had Glyn Morris with me.

... Lampl, Lawrence, Mann, Meade, Morris ...

That was him – my old mate from Reigate Grammar. He had gone on from there to Cranfield Business School and Harvard Business School, and then got a job with Rand McNally, the maps people, as an accountant. Then I recruited him for the Sutton Company. He came in and basically ran the numbers. It was comforting to have him around.

The company continued to strike out for a while longer, though. We took a long hard look at a company near Pittsburgh that made crockery, before we were outbid. That consumed a number of weeks. The point is, you usually need to examine a lot of different situations before you find something that makes sense. Loads of people at that early stage of the game will only be looking at one situation, and that's a recipe for disaster. In the end you've got to understand the risk involving the acquisition as fully as you possibly can, using all the data you can assemble. You do the homework until the numbers squeak, and you work out whether the risks are worth taking. At the Sutton Company we would look very hard at stuff before we bought it. We were bringing a rigour to that aspect of the process that I had learned at the Boston Consulting Group. Maybe that meant we weren't as fast out of the traps as others. On the other hand, we did 13 deals in the 14 years of the Sutton Company, most of which were add-ons, and they were all successfully integrated.

While we're on the subject of spending time on deliberation, it's probably also worth mentioning that I had a whole decade of experience behind me before I broke out and did my own thing. Maybe I'm cautious, but I think you're better off getting some experience rather than piling straight into your big solo effort. You hear about people who hit the jackpot straight off the bat – Bill Gates, Mark Zuckerberg – and you can get super rich that way. But the thousands who don't make it you don't hear about.

Nevertheless, even I would have to concede that there's biding your time and there's drifting towards the point of no return, which is where the Sutton Company found itself as those first 21 months went by and the big opening deal failed to land. Goodbye to the apartment in Beekman Place, then. That had to go – which was a wrench, but at least I made a huge profit on it. Six years after I had bought it for $58,000, it went for $350,000. In this I was the direct beneficiary of the city's bounce-back from its seventies decrepitude. Thank you for your service, Mayor Ed Koch.

I moved instead to a smaller, rented place in Dag Hammarskjöld Tower on 2nd Avenue. That was a very fancy address to have because, again, I didn't want anyone getting the wrong impression. But I wondered whether I had made a big mistake when, on one of my first nights in residence, I was woken in the middle of the night by pounding rock music coming from an apartment above me. It was the unmistakable sound of the Rolling Stones, with the voice of Mick Jagger to the fore.

Really? At four in the morning?

Outraged, I rang down to the concierge.

'Can you get them to turn off that Stones music?'

There was a pause. Then he said, 'That *is* the Rolling Stones.'

I said, '*What?*'

He said, 'Yeah, Keith Richards just moved into the building. They're up there.'

As I mentioned already, I was always more of a Beatles man myself. In fairness, though, the music cut out very shortly afterwards. I did see Keith Richards in the lift a few times. He would be coming in as I was leaving for work. But I never confronted him about that night. You want to stay on the right side of your neighbours.

The rent on a decent apartment aside, the only thing I treated myself to in those months of struggling was disability insurance. Not the most exciting thing to spend your money on, it's true. But I was haunted by the prospect of getting sick or getting injured in some way and being unable to work. So I took out a policy which would pay out $5,000 a month for the rest of my life in the event that something ruinous happened. And to the extent that afterwards I could sleep at night (Keith Richards and his pals permitting), it was a good investment.

In January 1984 came our empty-handed emergence from that court room in Poughkeepsie, with two New York families obliviously waging their long-standing turf war behind us. And then eight further months passed before that last throw of the dice on the shore of Lake Washington in Seattle, which is where we were when this book opened.

I thought I was practically insulting Furman Moseley with that offer for Simpson's building materials distribution business. I offered to pay book for the company, and also asked Moseley to take back $4 million of paper. In other words, he took a subordinated loan. As far as the bank was concerned, that was treated as equity. I was overjoyed when Moseley agreed to it.

I did, however, give a personal guarantee for a significant part of my net worth, ensuring that, if the thing got into trouble, the bank could come after me personally. True, in the event of a bankruptcy situation, there were probably enough assets in the company we were buying to cover the bank loan. Even so, signing that guarantee felt pretty sweaty. Glyn Morris, as chief financial officer, had to sign one, too. It was for a lot less than mine, but it was still a big commitment. All the paperwork was on the table, ready for our signatures, when Glyn suddenly got up, asked to be excused and left the room. I sat there for a while making polite conversation with the company's lawyers and the bank people. Time ticked on and Glyn failed to return. Eventually I ran out of polite conversation. Still no Glyn.

I was actually now a little worried about him. Maybe he had passed out or something. So then it was my turn to ask to be excused and I left to look for him.

I found him loitering, inside one of the stalls in the gents.

'What are you doing?' I said. 'They're waiting to close the deal.'

Glyn gave me a baleful look. I think he thought that if he stayed in the gents long enough, everyone would forget about his personal guarantee and the deal would get clinched without it. Or maybe he thought that eventually he would wake up and none of this would be happening to him. Whatever, I gently took him by the elbow and steered him out of the stall and back to the table, where, to everybody's relief but mostly mine, he signed.

So now, finally, the Sutton Company was out of the blocks. And of course the real work was only just beginning. There was no time to bask in that success. We were pitched straight into the fight. When you take over a company that is losing its shirt, it's automatically a race against time. You've got to move quickly and turn the thing around before the shirt is off completely, and your shirt with it.

The guy who had been managing things for Simpson's didn't want to continue under our ownership, so I had to step in. But that was a good thing because I could stir the pot in ways that he might have been reluctant to. It was clear that in order to build this company up, the first thing we needed to do, perhaps counter-intuitively, was scale the operation down. We closed a distribution centre out on the West Coast and concentrated our energies on everything that the company possessed east of the Rockies. It was a distribution business, so I rode in the trucks to see how we delivered stuff and I went out with the salesmen to see how we did the selling. I got into the guts of the business, which is what you have to do.

Meanwhile we were applying the fruits of the analysis that I had done in consultation with my pal Fred Nock who had been at BCG with me. There was one area in particular in which we knew we could turn the business around. When we took over, the company was paying its salesmen on gross margin, which is to say they received a commission which was a percentage of sales minus cost of goods sold. That's pretty standard. However, the company was losing money on a full-cost basis on a lot of the products it was selling. The salesmen were making money on those products all right, but the company was losing money.

And those products tended to be what we called the commodity products: such as 4 x 2s, plywoods – the bog-standard, unglamorous items in the range. Maybe half our products were commodities and the other half were specialities – the high-value products: such as windows, redwood, cedar and hardwood plywood.

So one obvious thing to do was to refocus the product line so that we sold the high-value specialities and not the commodities. The way we did it was to rethink the way we paid the salesmen. So we did some calculations in which we went way beyond the gross margin, factoring in the cost of carrying inventory, the cost of receivables, the cost of distribution – everything involved in getting that product to the customer. Instead of gross margin, we did a full cost analysis for each individual product in the range. And we came up with something called 'salesman's margin'. The principle was that the salesman's incentive would be completely aligned with our profit. When the salesman was making money, the company would be making money, in the same proportion. So instead of being evenly rewarded for sales across the product range, the salesman would be better remunerated for selling the higher-value products. This, naturally, would incentivize him to sell more of the higher-value products. This caused a lot of screaming and yelling among the salesmen when it was first put to them. 'We can't do that! We have to sell commodities to sell specialties.' But six months later, salesmen being salesmen, they had figured out a way. They were selling those higher-value products like never before and the commodities were way down and they were earning more money than ever before. As were we. And because our salesmen started earning so much, we started attracting the best salesmen – the perfect virtuous circle.

I should say that this was no easy win, though. It needed massaging. And that brings me to the point that there are two things involved in this game. The first is figuring out what to do with the business; the second, and more difficult, is persuading a bunch of guys to do it. Especially if they don't want to do it, which is probably most of the time, because people are actively resistant to change and feel threatened by it, especially when it's some new bloke stepping in and making the changes. That aspect of the job is called general management. And that's a darned sight harder than consulting.

Thirteen months after acquiring our first company, and with the turnaround beginning to take effect, we looked at buying an add-on business in Chicago – a company called Hines, which was also in building materials distribution but was bigger than our first acquisition. The notion was to blend the two businesses together, but first of all we needed to persuade the owners of Hines to sell to us. I flew out to Chicago a number of times during that phase with David Elenowitz, an aggressive and ebullient New Yorker who had joined the company as a partner. David had been in management consultancy with Bain in Boston, and he was good at strategy, a good financial guy – good all round. I can't overstate that one of the reasons the Sutton Company succeeded was that I managed to hire outstanding people

– people who really knew what they were doing and were highly motivated through having equity in the deals. Call it luck if you like, but I prefer to consider it judgement. Mind you, David wore me out from time to time, coming at me constantly to renegotiate his deal, his bonus, his equity ... He wouldn't let up. Once he was going off at me in the street about getting a bigger share of the equity in a deal we were doing and I was relieved when I reached the doorway to my apartment building. Now I could escape him. Not so fast. As I headed through the revolving door, David jammed it, trapping me in there, and continued haranguing me. The man was relentless.

Anyway, at the point at which we were negotiating with Hines, money was still tight, so David and I would fly out to Chicago using an awful discount airline. But we didn't want anybody knowing that. So our flight would arrive in its own sweet time and then we would linger in the baggage hall and wait for the far more dignified American or United flight to come in, and only then head into town. The Hines people would say, 'Did you have a good flight?' And we would say, 'Oh, yes. Came in on the American ...'

Appearances again. It was all part of the same theme: the right office, the right notepaper, the right home address, the right airline ... Ridiculous, really. Yet it was clear to me that, in America, the quickest way to fail in business was to look as though you were failing in business.

It was the same game a little while later, when we were trying to buy a company based in Belmont, Surrey. The company's two top guys agreed to meet us in the city. I flew in with David and rented the most expensive suite in the Savoy, a really incredible set of rooms with huge windows overlooking the Thames. David, meanwhile, had to content himself with a cheap shoebox at a hotel somewhere up the road. At the appointed time we met the company's people in the lobby area at the Savoy, where I was able to say, 'Look, it's not very private here, why don't we go up to my suite?' And straight away those people were thinking, 'Wow, these guys have got some money.' Which we didn't. Indeed, we had even less than we'd had a short while before, on account of the absurd price of the Savoy suite. OK, we didn't end up buying the company. But we sure as hell looked impressive while we weren't buying it.

Anyway, the most important asset of the Hines business in Chicago was that it had the franchise for Andersen windows for Chicagoland – a wonderful product and, if you knew about these things, which I made it my business to do, absolutely the top of the line among wooden windows. We made maintaining that franchise a condition of the sale, because we knew how valuable it was in the overall mix. Of course, that needed the agreement of Andersen themselves. They were a privately owned American-Swedish family business, and in order to be honoured with the right to sell their windows, you had to go to St Paul, Minnesota, on a diplomatic mission, go round the factory saying how marvellous it was and have a dinner with the family. And the whole time those guys would be looking at you to see whether you'd got two heads or were in any other way disreputable. We were on our best behaviour and they gave us the franchise, so the sale went ahead.

Once again, now that the acquisition was made, the hard work was just starting. I brought Don Hoffman on board, a talented accounts and finance guy with whom I had worked at International Paper. As with the Seattle operation, we initially trimmed the company back, cutting out some of the centres that were clearly beyond resuscitation. Closing places down is never a nice thing to do. And it's especially not a nice thing to do when the manager of the place that you're closing down has got a loaded shotgun leaning against his desk. This happened at a distribution centre in Wichita, Kansas. We had run the figures through the system and there was absolutely no way this part of the operation was ever going to start turning a profit. So I flew in to let the manager down as gently as possible. Nervously eyeing the lethal firearm off to one side, I began to mutter something about how there was no easy way to say what I had to say – which was especially true when there was a weapon in the room.

The manager interrupted me. 'Peter,' he said, 'I've thought this place was doomed for a long time.'

So at least it wasn't a surprise. And at least we agreed. And at least he didn't reach for the gun.

As before with the Seattle company, we switched the sales arrangement from gross margin to salesman's margin. And we moved the company's head office from Wilkes-Barre in Pennsylvania to Skokie, just north of Chicago, and Glyn Morris, who lived close by, went in to work on the premises. Now, those premises weren't exactly executive standard. The delivery trucks used to come in right below the office window, which meant that Glyn spent his working days wreathed in diesel fumes. As for the on-site bathroom facilities … well, essentially these were lavatories for warehousemen and truck drivers – truck-stop toilets. To muster the nerve to venture through that bathroom door, you would need to go very badly.

Glyn was constantly on at me. 'Can't we at least fix up the crappers?'

I was less than sympathetic. 'We don't have any money.'

Which was true. We still hadn't sold anything. Only a year or so later, when we were selling the Seattle and Chicago businesses together, did I think it might be a reasonable moment to revisit the Skokie toilet situation. After all, we were about to start showing potential buyers around, and it's the first rule of selling anything solid: first impressions count for everything. Now, I wasn't going to go as far as piping the smell of freshly baked bread through the building or standing baskets of fruit around the place, but I did at least think it might be a wise economy to fix up the bathrooms. Otherwise, what if one of the potential buyers asked to use the loo? As Glyn would vouch, the deal would be off before you could say, 'What exactly *is* that stain?'

So we sent in the builders and a complete lavatory revamp took place. The builders did a very fine job, too. I'm not sure that a warehouse in Skokie had ever seen such beautiful crappers. You could have sent the Queen of England in there without blushing.

As a result, we were all perfectly at ease when the first party of buyers turned up. We put them up at the Orrington, an upmarket hotel next to the Northwestern campus, and held the discussions away from our premises, in the hotel's more salubrious surroundings. But then we took them over to the offices for a visit, where we were completely relaxed at the prospect of somebody needing to use the bathroom. In fact, it was quite disappointing when that first party passed in and out of the building and nobody needed to go.

Never mind. There would be another bunch along in a while. Except that nobody in the second party needed to use the bathroom either.

By the time three groups of potential buyers had gone through without needing to heed nature's call, I was officially vexed. What was going on with these people's bladders?

'Jesus, Glyn, we spent all that money and nobody has even gone in there to wash their hands!'

By the time the fourth and fifth groups were going around, we were actively egging them on. 'Are you sure you don't need the restroom?' Still no takers.

By the time the sixth group arrived, I had pretty much given up and written off the investment in clean porcelain as a straight loss. I should have had more faith. As we walked around, the buyers' head guy suddenly said the three little words we had been longing to hear.

'Where's the bathroom?'

I restrained myself from leaping out of my chair and shouting 'Yes!', which would probably have been confusing.

And guess who ended up buying the operation? The sixth group – the one with the guy who took a leak.

The strategy lesson here: always clean up the bathrooms.

We sold those crappers and everything that came with them to a go-go British outfit which, in this period, seemed to be making acquisitions every week – Bunzl, a company which, coincidentally, my grandfather had worked for in Batley in Yorkshire after the war. Bunzl made it an absolute condition of sale that Don Hoffman stayed on in Chicago to keep an eye on things for two years. Don's wife didn't really like Chicago very much, so the whole deal trembled in the balance for a while. Fortunately she was persuaded to stay.

Don would eventually go down in Sutton Company legend during the week in Jamaica with which we marked our tenth anniversary, during which Don wore shorts with a pair of long black nylon socks. That sight would prove hard to shake. In the meantime, it was smart of Bunzl to keep Don involved. Their acquisitions people made a big mistake in another area, though: they didn't make holding onto the franchise for Andersen windows a condition of the sale. I don't know whether their people failed the rigorous personality test up at St Paul, or whether they were a little arrogant and casual about it, or what happened, but Andersen took the franchise away from them straight after the sale and bestowed it elsewhere. Without that franchise, that Chicago business was going to be very hard work. It seemed crazy to me that Bunzl hadn't realized that and put a condition of sale on it. Still, it was their problem now.

For that first Sutton sale, in which we bundled up our two initial acquisitions and sold them together, our lawyers were Skadden Arps, the premier mergers and acquisitions firm in New York.* I wouldn't have got them without Donald Brennan at Morgan Stanley putting in a word on my behalf with one of their top partners, Peter Atkins. Not that they cut me any slack. Skadden essentially looked me up and down and said: 'We'll represent you, but it's going to cost you.' Indeed. We negotiated a flat fee that was so high that my eyes watered for about a week afterwards. But it's what Skadden can get away with. Everybody wants them. They know the ropes, they have outstanding people, they're always on the end of deals, they do a huge volume of this stuff, and the more you do, the better you get at it. Consequently their reputation goes before them, and that's the reason I paid the premium rather than picking someone cheaper out of the phonebook. It put me on the front foot straight away. It was like walking in flanked by bodyguards. The guys opposite were going, 'Oh, my goodness – he's got Peter Atkins at Skadden.'

During the sale process, I was working like hell. For some time I had made it my practice to get in to the office at 6.45 in the morning, ready to start work at 7.00. But in

---

* Skadden, Arps, Slate, Meagher, Flom, to give them their full name, which, understandably, people tend not to. In 2015 Skadden Arps became the first law firm to advise on more than $1 trillion worth of deals in a single year. I don't think any of us needs to worry whether they're keeping their heads above water these days.

the lead-up to the sale, I was starting work at 4.00 in the morning and working through until 8.00 at night, when I would go and get a burger from somewhere and then go home and crash. And then it was up in the morning, shower and repeat. This went on for several weeks.

One time when I was coming into the building, the night doorman approached me.

'Tell me,' he said conspiratorially in a half-whisper, although there was nobody around to hear him, 'is it a … stock deal?'

He said the words 'stock deal' with great relish.

'Yeah,' I said. 'It's a stock deal.'

The caretaker let out a long, drawn-out 'Wooh!' And then he slowly walked away.

Only in New York. Did he even know what a stock deal was? I have no idea. But 'Wooh!' was exactly right. I don't think any of us had anticipated quite how big this deal was going to be. In December 1986, our two acquisitions sold for a combined \$36 million. We had converted an initial equity investment of \$0.3 million to \$18 million on exit in just two and a half years.

When the price of the sale was finally agreed, both Skadden and Morgan Stanley were clearly annoyed that they hadn't made as much money as they might have done. Skadden wanted to up their fee retrospectively, complaining that Morgan Stanley were getting more out of it than they were. Morgan Stanley also seemed to think that I might like to revisit their fee in the light of the deal's success. I had to face them both down.

Donald Brennan wasn't impressed either by my suggestion that we might pay them after closing rather than at
closing. My lawyers had worked out that there would be a
big tax advantage. But Brennan's response was typically
swift and crisp. 'If we don't get paid at closing,' he said,
'there won't *be* closing.' As so often, he sounded very firm
and not a little terrifying. So I shelved that idea
immediately.

As for Glyn Morris, I think he was glad that he came out
of the bathroom and signed that personal guarantee. He
pocketed his share and left the Sutton Company to do his
own thing. Eventually he got involved in publishing fine
books and developed a business buying classic cars and
shipping them to the UK.

As we were contemplating the sale, I knew this was a
great deal for Furman so I thought he might take a reduction in his loan from $4 million to $3 million. That arrangement had been made a fair while ago, and $1 million was
but a drop in the ocean as far as a man like Moseley was
concerned … I couldn't help wondering if he would now
accept less. I flew back out to Seattle for a meeting, in
Moseley's downtown office this time, and asked him if he
would take $3 million.

And what do you know? The simple answer to that
question was: 'No.' Moseley would have his $4 million, as
agreed. Our relationship, I'm pleased to say, continued on
a friendly footing.

I know. You'll be thinking, 'What kind of cheeky …?' But
if you don't ask …

10

MAKING SOME MORE MONEY

Once you're up and running, it gets easier. You've exited an investment, so you've got capital for further investments, and you've got successful management experience. That makes you attractive to the banks. When they see that you're bringing your own money to the table, you will get more leverage. And you've got the beginnings of a track record. We were able to leverage 20:1. The fact that we were a management group was the clincher. We kept our heads, though. We continued to move extremely carefully, and in our own time.

In 1987, I opened a Sutton Company office in London, where Oliver Quick from Kleinwort Benson joined as a partner. I had actually offered the role to a guy who was a vice-president of Scott Paper. He was due to start on the Monday, but on the Sunday evening, completely out of the blue, he pushed a bunch of stuff through my letterbox saying he wasn't coming after all. I fumed for a while and started mentioning lawyers, but in the end I calmed down, moved on and approached Oliver. David Elenowitz and I had encountered him in dealings with Kleinwort Benson and been very impressed by him. He turned out to be another of the outstanding appointments to which the success of the Sutton Company owed so much, and he went on to become a trustee of the Sutton Trust.

Together, Oliver and I looked at a number of possible acquisitions in the UK, but none of them felt right to us and we ended up leaving them all alone. Most of the deals on offer were management buy-outs, meaning that the existing management were getting much too big a piece of the action. Because of this we couldn't get the numbers to work, so we walked away.

I often reflect on how lucky I was to have been in New York when I wanted to get the Sutton Company off the ground. I don't think it would have been possible in London at that time. London didn't seem to be geared up for leveraged buy-outs in the way that New York was. It was playing catch-up. Banking still felt stiff and starchy – stuck in a colonial, bowler-hat-and-rolled-umbrella past. I remember going into the offices of Standard Chartered in London one time and crossing a room which was filled with women seated at desks arranged in ranks, tapping away silently at calculators. The manager took us into his office, sat us down and asked if we would like a cup of coffee. We said that would be very nice. He then returned to his office door, leaned out and shouted at the top of his voice, 'Two cups of sludge!' That seemed to sum it up somehow.

By contrast, in New York, you would go to Bear Stearns and not only was there quite good coffee, there was a tangible can-do energy in the room. Or alternatively a tangible *can't*-do energy, because those guys would have no compunction about showing you the door if they didn't like what you were asking for. Also, those American banks would see you the next day. You would ring up Rothschild's in London and consider yourself lucky if they could see you within a week. At that time, the London banking scene was much less driven and far more suspicious and circumspect, and I suspect it would have suffocated the Sutton Company at birth.

What the London office did was provide a platform for moving into Germany, which we were extremely keen to do. I had seen, while at the Boston Consulting Group, how the Mittelstand, the small and medium-sized privately owned German firms, were very often good businesses, and I felt I had a strong connection there. But, again, there was no hurry. Having settled the company into premises in Hill Street, off Berkeley Square (close to Citibank's HQ and Annabel's nightclub, in keeping with that Sutton Company philosophy about prestigious addresses), we didn't make our first European acquisition until two years later, in 1989. That was a German company called Krings.

What Krings did was supply the construction industry with shoring systems for trenches. Now, perhaps by this point you are noticing a theme: everything we bought at the Sutton Company was as boring as hell. Deliberately so.

It became a litmus test, actually: would this business put people to sleep at a cocktail party? If the answer was 'yes', then it was a good business for the Sutton Company. Krings certainly passed the all-important cocktail party test. 'I'm in the shoring systems business.' Trust me, when you said that at a party, people were practically climbing over the canapés to get away from you.

This wasn't just perversity, though: there was some thought behind this system. The market for businesses that were making seemingly glamorous and exciting things – like the latest technology, sunglasses, luxury boats, or whatever – was way more competitive. Fiercely so, in fact. People want to be associated with that kind of stuff – and are frequently willing to pay a premium to get involved in something they think is ritzy. They can lose perspective. With things like shoring systems and building materials distribution … well, those businesses tend not to go to people's heads in quite the same way. Economics determines success in those areas, not vanity. Just as we went for medium-sized companies that we knew we could get our hands and heads around, so we went all-out for boring companies – companies providing unglamorous services to unglamorous industries. It made sense. It was our particular strength.

Also, say what you like about shoring systems, but they're crucial. If you dig a trench while you're installing something like a sewage pipe, it stands to reason that you're going to need something to hold up the walls of that trench in case it collapses on your workmen. And Krings' shoring systems would turn out to do very well for us – far better than we had dreamed, in fact. We had, as usual, analysed the company and its potential in the marketplace as carefully as we could, and we felt we had a high chance of making the thing yield a high return. But there was one key factor that featured nowhere on our spreadsheets: the fall of the Berlin Wall.

The history books show that at 10.45 p.m. on 9 November 1989, the East German border guards, following government orders, opened the checkpoints along the Berlin Wall and stood back to let the East Berliners flood through them. The history books also show that just a few months before that, in June, the Sutton Company, using only $2.1 million of its own money and borrowing the rest, had acquired a company providing vital services to the German construction industry. Talk about being on the right side of history. One minute we're taking a measured assessment of the likely growth potential of a business that services building projects; the next, a soon-to-be-reunified country is looking to get the builders in.

Now, I would love to take the credit here for my uncanny instincts in relation to the ebbs and flows of European politics, but I would be lying through my teeth. Once again, it was all about those things economists call 'discontinuities'. You assume that life is going to bumble along much as it always has. And then something massive comes winging in which throws everything out of kilter. Suddenly there's a pandemic, say, or the Berlin Wall falls, or Brexit happens, or a reality show television personality somehow gets elected President of the United States. In business, you can do all the homework you like, but you will always ultimately be at the mercy of things beyond your control. As Harold Macmillan described it, 'Events, my dear boy, events!' In this case, we could only count our blessings that world affaris had swung things resoundingly our way.

When we bought Krings, it was run from Heinsberg near Aachen by two German businessmen: Herr Hutz, who owned the majority of the equity, and Herr Rhyssen (later known to us as Dieter), who owned the rest. Dieter was a formidable, fast-living, fast-driving figure whom I liked immensely, even if sitting beside him while he tore his hot BMW up a German autobahn at close to 150mph will qualify as one of the most frightening experiences of my life. The workers on site always seemed pleased to see him, and no wonder: he was always pressing rolls of notes on the foreman as he left, saying, 'Buy the boys a beer.'

Dieter stayed on to help us run Krings as chief executive, though that was a close thing. Dresdner, the German bank that was funding the purchase, needed him to have a medical, just to be sure that he was going to be around for a while after the deal was struck. Naturally, those of us on the buy side were concerned for both Dieter and the future of the deal when the medical report came back less than sparkling. The condition of Dieter's liver in particular seemed to be troubling the specialists. Dieter couldn't have cared less, though. He simply went and got another, more satisfactory report from somewhere else. I'm still not sure how he managed that. But it satisfied Dresdner.*

Dieter also had an interesting philosophy in relation to note-taking during business negotiations. He used to say, 'If you tell the truth, you never need to write anything down. It's only when you're lying that you need to take notes.' This was a sound piece of practical wisdom, although it also meant that you were always instantly worried when you spotted Dieter beavering away with a pen during meetings.

At closing, Hutz chose to become very difficult, arguing anew over reps and warranties, and throwing all sorts of stumbling blocks in the path of the deal. At two in the morning we took a break. I was quietly steaming, because I had started to wonder, in the face of all these new and, to my mind, piffling obstructions, whether the deal would ever close. At this point, as I took some deep breaths and tried to retain my composure, the guy from Dresdner Bank, Herr Weinmann, reached into his inside pocket and took out a cheque for the purchase price, which he passed over to me. I was gobsmacked. Bankers don't normally carry around cheques for the sums involved in buying a company. That kind of thing normally only happens on game shows. You know: 'Take a look at what you might be winning!'

---

* In defence of the specialists behind that first medical verdict, Dieter sadly died about seven years after this episode. However, in equal defence of the specialists behind the second medical verdict, this was well outside the binding terms of the bank deal. Indeed, it was after we had sold the company and repaid the loan.

'Show it to Hutz,' I said to Herr Weinmann. 'Just show it to him.'

By now, I was ready to try almost anything – including game-show tactics. When the meeting resumed, Weinmann took out the cheque and waved it in front of Hutz. He looked down at the piece of paper with the figures on it and his eyes widened. And what do you know? All those little objections he had been having melted clean away. He saw the money – and the deal closed. He pocketed the cheque and we shook hands heartily. Then we all got our coats and got out of there as fast as we could.

Dieter Rhyssen looked as though he had never had any doubt about it. 'He's going straight home to show that to his girlfriend,' he said sagely.

The sale of Krings in April 1992 saw the value of that company almost triple and produced $27 million profit for the Sutton Company. It enabled us, two months later, to purchase another German company, SKS, which specialized in roller shutters and balconies for apartment buildings. The market for both those products in the former East Germany, where thousands upon thousands of buildings were being smartened up after years of neglect, was stupendous. Our $3.3 million of equity became $80 million when we sold SKS almost exactly five years later, in July 1997.

Kasia Robinski joined the company, working briefly in the London office and then heading over to New York to look into deals for us in the US. A Cambridge graduate and Stanford Business School MBA who had been working for

Goldman Sachs, Kasia was an ideas dynamo. Memos and emails from her with thoughts and suggestions would arrive on my desk at the rate of virtually one every ten minutes. It was like machine-gun fire. Kasia remains a good friend and continues to be valuably dynamic on the Sutton Trust board.

Meanwhile, back in the US, we had bought a company called LaSalle-Deitch, which was based in Elkhart, Indiana, and was a specialty distributor to the mobile home and recreational vehicle industries. I have to say this company performed strongly in the send-'em-packing-at-a-party test. Elkhart was the home of the American recreational vehicle and mobile home industry and LaSalle-Deitch supplied products for the classic kind of wallowy, road-filling leisure vehicles that tend to have bumper stickers on the back saying things like, 'If the box is rockin', don't come knockin'.' Basically, the Sutton Company was now in the wobbly box business. I remember the motto of our salesmen was: 'It ain't easy being sleazy.'

Among the perks, apart from all the bumper stickers you could ever pine for, was a set of 16 seats at Notre Dame college football games. College football at Notre Dame was a huge deal, and those were highly covetable tickets. They came in especially handy when we were selling the business and were able to invite prospective buyers to come along for a day of tail-gating in the car park – that great institution of American sports-going where people tip up early for the game, sling open the boots of their cars and feast on barbecue and beers for the day. Joe Ellis, who sold the business to us, bought himself the biggest RV in the Notre Dame car park, a vehicle so big it practically had its own zip code.

We kept LaSalle for five years, improved earnings substantially and sold it for $65 million.

So, now I personally had a considerable amount of money in the bank. Does money change people? How could it not?

What happens is that you start putting down to skill the things that came to you by luck. The business world is full to bursting with people who got a lucky break and then began attributing it to their own personal genius. I guess I wrestled to a greater or lesser extent with all of these standard delusions in the first flush of wealth. But I will say this much for myself: I don't think I ever lost sight of the fact that I had got lucky.

For four years, as I struggled to get the company up and running, I was really up against it, and then suddenly, in a rush, money was no object. One of the first things I treated myself to was a BMW 7 Series, the biggest saloon in the BMW range, and had it kitted out with a 'fuzz buster' which detected radar and let you know when the police were around. As a consequence of one of the Sutton Company's acquisitions, we had our main office in Wilkes-Barre, Pennsylvania, and I drove there and back every week from New York. It took about two and a half hours each way and I would take that car close to 100mph up the fabulous roads across the Delaware Gap, feeling quite the executive racing driver. If the police were in the area, the fuzz buster would sound and I would slam on the brakes. I loved that car.

In 1987, wanting a London base, I acquired 71 Chester Square in Belgravia. Chester Square is flanked with nineteenth-century white stucco terraces, and number 71 is a key house, in the middle of the terrace and wider than the other houses. It's arguably one of the prime houses in London, at one of the most prestigious addresses, and it cost me £1.6 million. That place is probably worth £30 million now.

When Margaret Thatcher was removed from office in 1990, she moved one door away from me, to number 73. Life in Chester Square got interesting at that point. I would go to play golf at the weekend and invariably Denis Thatcher would be out on the street, polishing his Rolls. I would come back a few hours later, and he would still be out there polishing.

And there was 24-hour police protection on guard at the front and back of the building. There was something enormously reassuring about that. Mind you, heading out of the front door at the crack of dawn one morning, when it was still dark, I trod on something large and soft on the doorstep and promptly took an absolute purler into the street.

It was a policewoman.

'Please,' she said, scrambling up off the floor and smoothing herself down, 'don't tell anyone. I'll get fired.'

It had been tipping down with rain all night and she had apparently taken shelter in my porch, where she had fallen sound asleep. (Mrs Thatcher's place didn't have a covered porch and mine did ...)

Lady Thatcher, as she became, lived on at that address until she died in 2013. I had long since sold up. But during my tenure, as a neighbourly gesture, I dropped her a line to tell her who I was and what I was doing, which, by that stage, was running the Sutton Trust and agitating for increased social mobility. And she, in an equally neighbourly fashion, invited me round for drinks. So round I went, somewhat nervously.

I perched on a chair, nursing a glass containing a generous slosh of whisky. Sitting opposite, with an equally well-filled glass, Lady Thatcher seemed to take great pleasure in informing me that the chair I was sitting on had once been occupied by 'my great friend General Pinochet'.*

That didn't put me any more at my ease. Lady Thatcher and I had Oxford University in common, of course, although she now hated the place because it hadn't seen fit to give her an honorary degree. Something else we shared: our choice of degree subject. As soon as I arrived, she pounced on me and said, 'Oh, Mr Lampl, I'm so glad you read chemistry. Chemistry is a *proper* degree – not like PPE, which is just common sense.'†

---

* General Augusto Pinochet, the Chilean dictator to whom, despite his human rights record, Lady Thatcher controversially felt loyal on account of his assistance behind the scenes during the Falklands War.

† PPE – philosophy, politics and economics – is an Oxford degree subject popular with future politicians. A number of the politicians who had stabbed her in the back had read PPE.

Denis was there, too, on a break, apparently, from polishing his car, and I seem to recall him muttering from time to time about things being 'all the bloody unions' fault'. Sadly, I can't recall *what* things were all the bloody unions' fault. Take your pick, I guess.

Anyway, my circumstances had transformed exponentially. And as if to underscore that point, quite by coincidence, the Sutton Company during one phase in this period found itself looking at buying Dowty's mining division in Cheltenham, the division that my father had worked for. He had just retired, and the deal didn't come off in any case. But as we researched it, it was interesting to hear, from someone who had been there at the same time as my dad, of his influence on the company. He still seemed very well regarded there for his work as Export Marketing Director, flying out as a trouble-shooter to wherever in the world there was an engineering problem, rolling up his sleeves and sorting it out. He was enthusiastically received wherever he went. You realize that that's what people really like: someone who can fix things, who can put stuff right that's broken. People will always take that over someone who's trying to sell them something.

It was also revealed to me that my dad would go into Dowty board meetings with a pile of magazines to read. He didn't really see the point of board meetings. He thought all that talking was a waste of time. He didn't feel it was any substitute for doing stuff. For making a difference that people could see. He wasn't wrong about that, either.

11

DUNBLANE AND AFTER

I took a lot of satisfaction from what I had achieved in a short space of time with the Sutton Company. I had come from nowhere, starting with nothing. And 12 years later, by a combination of a touch of entrepreneurial daring, good analysis and management, some extremely fortuitous timing and just sheer dumb luck, I was worth over £100 million. I was only in my late forties, yet I had put myself in a position where, if I wanted to, I could retire and devote the rest of my life to really important things, such as tennis and golf.

And actually, as it turned out, both tennis and golf did get more of my attention in this period. For instance, I did the grand slam, ticking off the four tennis majors as a punter: the Australian Open in Melbourne in January, the French Open in Paris in May, Wimbledon in July and the US Open at Flushing Meadows in August. The best of these? It's got to be the French Open. It's in a charming location in the Bois de Boulogne and the long, gruelling rallies, courtesy of the clay, are mesmerizing. My favourite player at the time was Mats Wilander, from Sweden. This was 1988, when he won three out of those four grand slam tournaments. If he had won at Wimbledon, he would have pulled off the fabled 'calendar slam' – the same as me. I thought Wilander was magical. He wasn't possessed of the greatest physical attributes, but he had a tenacious ability to outthink his opponents.

As for golf, around about this time a friend told me places were opening at Wentworth in Surrey. This sounded tempting. In the late 1990s and early 2000s, Wentworth was bought and sold a couple of times and somewhere in the middle of all that, I would suggest, it lost its soul and became a golf factory. But at this point, Wentworth was still a members' club. The place had an undeniable allure, what with its standing in the history of the game (the first home, in 1926, of the competition that would become the Ryder Cup, no less), its azalea-lined driveway and castellated nineteenth-century clubhouse, and its position at the heart of a ritzy residential estate featuring the houses of golf pros and showbiz stars. Admirably or otherwise, something in me twitched at the possibility of becoming a part of it.

Just two problems: first, Wentworth had an 18-handicap cut-off for members; second, I didn't play golf.

Still, here was an incentive to learn – and to learn properly. So I submitted my application and told myself that in six months' time I would be in a position to play the round with the club captain that was part of the entry process. During that time I enrolled for numerous *Golf Digest-*

endorsed golf schools, which are generally considered the best in America. As the deadline approached, my game was starting to get into pretty good shape. And so it should have been, given the money I had lavished on it. Nevertheless, the big question was, would it hold up under pressure on the big day, under the scrutiny of the Wentworth club captain? Or would the members boot me straight back up their azalea-lined driveway at the first sight of my recently born swing?

The day dawned. There I was, the captain alongside me, teeing it up at the first on the East Course – a relatively gentle introduction to life at Wentworth, certainly by contrast with the West Course, where whole acres of rough seem to spread out in front of you before you even reach the fairway. Nevertheless, on that first hole, everything I had been so expensively taught seemed to desert me under the captain's steely gaze. My drive veered off in the direction of London and I was extremely fortunate to recover and make bogey. But, to my relief, the captain bogeyed the hole, too. Nothing to be embarrassed about yet, then. We moved on, my membership still very much in play.

The second hole featured a giant bunker in the middle of the fairway – one of those that you either keep well short of or, in a fit of madness, take on. In the circumstances, the obvious thing to do was exercise extreme caution. That, at least, was what my brain was saying as I stood over my ball on the tee. However, the message didn't seem to get from my brain through to my body. I felt my arms bring the club down and then watched with astonishment as my ball flew high into the sky, right in the direction of the bunker – and cleared it, bouncing satisfyingly in the middle of the fairway beyond. I had hit the truest shot I had ever struck on a golf course in my life up to that point, and certainly a truer shot than any I have hit since. It was as if all those months of golf school in America had come together in that one stroke – and would never come together like that again, although that was a secret worth keeping from the captain at that point.

Perhaps inspired by my shining example, the captain also took the bunker on – and landed his ball in it. And that was it: game over. I was in.

So I was member at Wentworth, and I suppose there was little to stop me spending all my time thereafter whittling away at my handicap while the azaleas nodded gently in the Surrey breeze and Bruce Forsyth, or whoever, looked on. I can't pretend it wasn't tempting. It was certainly more tempting than opening up yet another stack of files and beginning to examine the pros and cons of yet another deal. In 1983, I had set up my company with an absolute hunger for that kind of work. Fourteen years and 13 deals later (and with a lot of money in the bank), I couldn't deny it: the pleasure seemed to be wearing thin.

The Sutton Company could have run on and on, if we had chosen to let it. True, a number of factors might have tripped us up. We might have been swiped aside by a global crash that was entirely beyond our control. Or we might have taken a disastrous mis-step somewhere along the way, made a misguided investment decision. But recklessness wasn't in the company's DNA and over-reaching was something we had carefully schooled ourselves against. As far as anything could be predicted, it was reasonable to assume that we could sail on as we had been: slowly, steadily, biding our time, doing the research, picking the right vehicle, improving the profitability and then exiting the investment.

But did I want to be doing leveraged buy-outs for the rest of my life? More particularly, did I want to be doing leveraged buy-outs now that I had enough money not to have to? I found that having made a lot of money was demotivating. Yes, there was the challenge of managing the companies that we acquired and improving their performance. And yes, that was absorbing and involving and there was a sense of achievement to be taken from it. But at the same time, you're looking to exit that business as soon as you think its valuation has increased substantially enough. And as unsentimental as it sounds, the day you exit a company is the day you forget all about it. And then you're on to the next one.

Where do you stop, though? That was a question that was increasingly on my mind as the 1980s turned into the 1990s. Once you have started making money, there are pressures to continue doing so, and they're not necessarily coming from inside yourself. In the business world, money is the way people keep score. You are judged by how much money you have, and it starts to be how you rank yourself, too. And for a short while, in my thirties, with things to prove, that might have seemed a game worth playing. But now, in my late forties, the truth was I found it boring. As

I looked around at other people in my position, still working away, I thought: 'If you're worth all that money, why are you still killing yourself?' What was the point? I had made more than I was ever going to be able to spend. I had satisfied the obvious urges: the nice places to live, the nice cars. What next? A yacht? Not for me.

In 1987, two years after I had returned to live in London, I had met Karen Gordon. Karen was Canadian and she was working as a planning executive on my old stomping ground at Beecham's, which had become SmithKline Beecham. So we had that in common, and we seemed to have a lot more. We married in 1994, set up home together in Wimbledon, and started a family. And perhaps this is not surprising, but the time when I was having these thoughts about my future path coincided with the arrival of my children: my daughters, Katie in 1995 and Steph in 2000, and, between them, in 1997, my son, Chris. Children teach you to look beyond yourself in ways you haven't been doing. They change your sense of what's important. It can't be mere coincidence that those three small people came into my life at exactly the same time as the appeal of investigating the potential medium-term profitability of another business making shoring systems for use in buildings construction began to wane – at a point in my life when I was asking questions such as, 'How do I get out of this?' and 'Is there something out there I could more usefully be doing with all this money?'

* * *

On 13 March 1996, at 9.30 a.m., Thomas Hamilton, a 43-year-old former shopkeeper who now ran boys' clubs, walked into Dunblane Primary School near Stirling in Scotland. He had with him four legally owned handguns and 743 rounds of ammunition. He entered the Gymnasium, where Primary 1/13, a class of five- and six-year-olds, had just begun their lesson. In a little under four minutes he had used one of his guns, a 9mm Browning self-loading pistol, to fire 105 shots. He killed 16 schoolchildren and a teacher, and wounded ten other children and three further members of the teaching staff. He then used another of his guns to shoot himself.

The incident threw the country into shock. It was, in the stunned words of the Scottish MP Helen Liddell, 'a slaughter of the innocents, unlike anything we have ever seen in Scotland'.

Like everybody else in the UK, I was numb. I was numb, as any sentient person would be, at this brutal incursion into the safe space of a primary school. I was numb, as a resident of the United Kingdom. This kind of thing simply didn't happen here. Except that now it did.

And as well as being numb, I was fearful. My perspective was coloured by two decades of living in the States. I had always been perplexed and horrified by what went on there in relation to guns – what I had come to see as the complete madness of that country's relationship with firearms. I have a house in Florida and I have spent a lot of time there. In Florida they staged a celebration because the state was the first to reach the magic figure of 2 million concealed gun-carry permits, crushing Texas, which at the time had 'only' issued around 1.5 million permits. At the time of writing, the number of guns in America is well over 300 million and amounts to more than one gun per adult. You are as likely to die from gunfire in America as you are to die in a traffic accident in the UK. With the exception of the restrictive states of New York and California, gun-death appears to be a risk that Americans are simply pricing in, in the same way that some of us price in the risks of taking a car out on the road.

But it's not just the numbers of guns, and it's not just the numbers of people who are shot dead; it's the collateral impact that a gun-driven culture has on general life even when people aren't getting shot, and even when guns aren't visible or present – the constant low-level fear that the tacit acceptance of guns induces and somehow normalizes. It's the 'active shooter' drills in 100,000 American schools each week, it's the 'lock-down training' sessions in offices. What becomes of a society where those kinds of things are simply commonplace, part of the routine?

I have a Florida story which amounts to nothing in a sense, yet perfectly illustrates the grim way in which gun-induced anxiety spreads into the most mundane corners. I'm awake at 6.00 one Sunday morning and I decide to buy some donuts. Somewhere on the drive, on an otherwise deserted two-lane highway, a car goes past me, then brakes until I have overtaken it, then goes past me again. Then it brakes again and drops in behind me, following closely. After a while I make a U-turn to get to Dunkin' Donuts, which is on the other side of the road. The other car does the same. I turn into the car park. So does the car on my tail. I get out, and so does the pursuing driver.

He has road rage. 'You cut me off!' he screams.

Maybe I did cut him off somewhere back there, though I'm unaware of it. I'm terrified and I retreat into the store. But it doesn't end there. He comes in after me, still shouting. I realize that I am quivering – not because of the violence of the verbal assault, although that is something, but because of the one question that's been repeating in my mind throughout this episode: does this guy have a gun? How badly could this ridiculous moment escalate? Because people get shot in road-rage incidents all the time in Florida, triumphant home of the two millionth concealed gun permit.

Eventually, to my surprise and relief, the guy stops shouting at me and goes back to his car. Through the store window, I watch him pull away. And I am left to order a coffee and calm down, which takes at least half an hour. This, clearly, is one of the places where the right to bear arms casually leaves you: shaking with fear in Dunkin' Donuts at 6.30 on a Sunday morning.

In the weeks after Dunblane, I began to read in the paper about a newly formed pressure group called the Gun Control Network. These were lawyers, academics, the parents of children killed in Dunblane and relatives of victims of the 1987 shooting in Hungerford, where a 35-year-old man armed with a handgun and two semi-automatic rifles killed 16 and injured 15 in various places around the town before turning the handgun on himself. After Hungerford, the government had acted, but clearly an even stronger line could have been taken.* However, Britain at the time had had no organization focused on gun laws that could take the argument to the politicians and be a powerful force opposing the shooting lobby. In the wake of Dunblane, the Gun Control Network would be that missing organization. They were campaigning to ban private ownership of all handguns in the UK. To me, superficially, it seemed like an ambitious target – unlikely, frankly. But, at this potential tipping-point for British life, it also seemed essential.

I read everything that I could find on the Gun Control Network and then met up with Gill Marshall-Andrews, the founder of the organization. I explained that I was an entrepreneur who had some money and was fully in support of what she and the people alongside her were trying to achieve. I asked her to let me know if I could be of any use to her and her fellow campaigner Mick North. Mick had played a huge part in the Gun Control Network from the start. Over time, he emerged as the 'lead' parent in the handgun campaign and his contribution and commitment were enormous.

Gill came to see me at home, bringing with her two people who had lost family members to gun crime – one at

* The government passed the Firearms (Amendment) Act 1988, which made registration mandatory for shotgun ownership and banned high-powered self-loading rifles and burst-firing weapons. This was a long way short of a full firearms ban.

Dunblane, one at Hungerford. We sat down together in my living room. It was very emotional – a meeting unlike any I had ever had. They talked to me about what they had been through, the children they had lost and the circumstances in which they had lost them.

How do you begin to cope with that? How do you pick yourself up off the floor and carry on? And yet I could feel their drive and their conviction. I marvelled at the resolve that they had kindled and the purpose they now had. These were people who wanted to bring about significant change. But they knew that there were vast odds against them – that there were 200,000 legally registered handguns in Britain at that time and that there was a motivated and powerful pro-gun sports lobby that already felt it had been scapegoated in 1988, after Hungerford, and would firmly resist further restrictions on its freedoms. They knew there was a lot to take on.

Yet the cause was clearly urgent. Between 1984 and 1994, gun crime involving handguns in England and Wales had risen by 140 per cent – from 1,232 crimes in 1984 to 2,981 crimes in 1994. In each of those ten years, the handgun was the most common firearm used in robberies. The 9mm gun used by Thomas Hamilton was tested after the massacre and found to be capable of releasing a full magazine of 20 bullets in 5.46 seconds. It was self-evident: this thing needed shutting down.

I could see that there was an opportunity here, not simply to seek some tiny measure of redemption for the tragedies of Dunblane and Hungerford, but in some sense to alter the future direction of a culture. If we could get handguns banned completely, it would be a monumental achievement. I volunteered to fund the campaign.

The Gun Control Network went to work, lobbying politicians, raising public awareness, keeping the issue as high on the news agenda as they could. The government had commissioned Douglas Cullen to conduct the public inquiry into the events at Dunblane. Lord Cullen was a member of the Scottish judiciary and had conducted the inquiry into the Piper Alpha oil platform disaster of 1988. In the case of Dunblane, he heard 26 days of oral testimony and weighed a mountain of written submissions, and he filed his report on 30 September 1996, just over six months after the massacre. At the conclusion of that report he made 23 recommendations for tightening the rules on gun ownership and for monitoring those who work with children. But he stopped short of advocating a ban.

Cullen stated that he was prepared to recommend prohibiting high-calibre handguns, but only if his preferred recommendation – a stepped-up system for disabling certain guns and safely storing their component parts when they weren't in use – proved unworkable. 'The banning of multi-shot handguns,' he observed, 'would have a very damaging effect on the sport of target shooting.' He noted, somewhat feebly, that the estimated worth to the economy of that sport was £20 million.

From the campaign's point of view, Cullen's conclusions were bitterly disappointing – a limp compromise, designed to offer minor concessions to the anti-gun sector while at the same time amply placating the gun sports lobby. It was also clear by now that Cullen was out of step with the broader public feeling on this issue, which was strongly in favour of a ban. Capitalizing on that, the parallel Snowdrop Campaign, set up and led by a group of local mothers and fully supported by the Dunblane parents, gathered 750,000 signatures on a petition in favour of banning handguns and handed it in to Parliament, ensuring that the momentum for the ban continued to build. As part of the second phase of their campaigning, for the ban to include .22s, Snowdrop had also commissioned a powerful cinema advert, with a compelling voice-over by Sean Connery, in which a human-shaped target was blown apart by gunfire. The Labour opposition strongly advocated a total handgun ban and some on the Conservative side joined them in doing so. It didn't hurt the cause when the high-profile Tory MP David Mellor stood up in Parliament and said, 'Isn't it time to conclude that, literally and metaphorically, the game is up for handguns now?'

In due course, John Major's Tory government published its response to the Cullen report: 'The Government has decided to legislate early in the next session of Parliament to ban all hand guns of more than .22 calibre – including those used by Thomas Hamilton. This will mean that at least 160,000 guns – 80 per cent of those legally held at present – will be destroyed. All handguns chambered for .22 rimfire ammunition, including single-shot guns, will also be banned unless they are kept in licensed gun clubs under conditions of the most stringent security. This means that, in two important respects, the Government intends to go further than Lord Cullen's proposals: by banning all high-calibre handguns; and by prohibiting people from keeping even single-shot handguns at home.'*

Now, this was a triumph. But the best was yet to come. In May, Tony Blair was elected by a landslide and the Labour government very quickly put through legislation which banned the private ownership of all cartridge ammunition handguns, regardless of calibre.†

At this point, the campaign's founding mission had been accomplished: a complete ban on handguns. The UK could now boast that it had some of the strictest legislation on gun ownership and gun use in the world.

I watched all this develop with delight and relief, but from a distance. I can't pretend that my input was anything more than that of a typical funder. I wrote some cheques and I did so anonymously. I wasn't involved in a personal capacity and I had no input into the campaign's direction or strategy: I left it to the discretion of those who knew far more than I did. I was kept informed about what was going on, but the truth is, at the time I didn't really want anyone to know that I was involved. This was a very emotive issue. It stood to upset some people. If I had been out there in public, appearing in newspapers as the wealthy entrepreneur backing this campaign with his own cash, I have to confess I would have been worried for my own safety.

* All this was duly ratified in the Firearms (Amendment) Act 1997.

† The Firearms (Amendment) (No. 2) Act 1997.

Maybe I was a coward. Maybe I should have been prepared to put my head above the parapet. At the same time, there were a lot of unhappy people out there. A lot of unhappy people with guns.

Including, incidentally, my father. Somewhere in the attic of my parents' house, my dad had kept a German Luger pistol. It was something he had come by during combat in the war – a memento of those dark days.

Following the Blair government's legislation in 1997, there was an amnesty in which people could give up their arms without further questions. The Home Secretary, Michael Howard, got behind this, saying, 'Every gun that is removed out of people's homes and off the streets is one fewer potential threat, one less potential tragedy or one less potential crime.' And in September 1998, in a written reply to a question in the House of Lords, the Home Office Minister of State, Lord Mostyn, declared that 162,198 handguns had been surrendered since the Dunblane massacre, the vast majority of which had been destroyed.

Among those guns was the one handed in by my father. As a consequence of a campaign funded by his son, he had to clamber up in the roof, get down his now illegal weapon and hand it in at the police station. Ah well. My father never did like guns.

It took a little while for the effects of the ban to be properly felt. Gun crime continued to rise in Britain after Dunblane, reaching a peak of 24,094 offences involving guns in 2003/04. But then the numbers started to fall, and continued to fall annually. In 2010/11 there were 11,227 offences – 53 per cent below the peak figure. Crime involving handguns fell 44 per cent in that same period.

We had been moving towards a gun culture in Britain and I genuinely believe we would be someway towards an American state of affairs by now if it hadn't been for what happened after Dunblane. That post-Dunblane campaign was lastingly significant. It sent a message around the world about what governments in major countries could and would do in relation to gun legislation when the will was there. And it exceeded our brightest expectations. I was thinking, optimistically, that maybe the outcome of the campaign would be tighter rules on ownership, greater gun control. That in itself would have been a result to be celebrated. But no: in the end it was an outright ban.

In 2016, I was proud to host a party at the British Academy where friends of the Gun Control Network celebrated two decades of campaigning to change the law and the culture around guns in the UK. The achievements the organization could point to included, obviously, the complete ban on civilian handgun ownership in 1997, but also, since that, a ban in 2006 on the manufacture, import and purchase of realistic imitation guns, which followed a six-year-long campaign; a requirement, again made law in 2006, for airguns to be sold only through registered firearms dealers; changes in 2012 to firearms licensing, preventing people with a history of domestic violence, drug or alcohol abuse or mental illness from getting a gun licence; and in 2016 the establishment of a Gun Safety Line, run by Crimestoppers, enabling people to report concerns about gun owners. Over the years, the Gun Control Network has grown in power to become the UK's chief barrier against the always powerful shooting lobby.

When I try to tell Americans about this, they can't get their heads around it. 'A ban on all types of gun?' And I point out that the UK doesn't have a written constitution which protects its citizens' ability to carry handguns like the one wielded by Thomas Hamilton in Dunblane. In 2012, Americans were obliged to bear witness to the massacre at Sandy Hook Elementary School in Newtown, Connecticut, where 20 children aged between six and seven and six adult staff members were killed. At the time, America had a pro-gun control president, Barack Obama, who wanted to implement change and made concrete proposals to do so. And still nothing happened. Those proposals were batted back by US senators in hock to the National Rifle Association. If America wouldn't do it for the slaughtered children of Sandy Hook, it's hard not to conclude that America won't do it for anybody. Dunblane was Britain's Newtown, and Britain acted and closed the situation down. By contrast, in 2018, in the wake of the shooting of 17 people by a 19-year-old former student at Marjory Stoneman Douglas High School in Parkland, Florida, Trump listened to the testimony of school-shooting survivors and victims' parents, and addressed the eternal question 'What can be done?' by floating the notion of arming teachers. Really, where do you even begin with that?

In retrospect, funding the Gun Control Network campaign after Dunblane was, I suppose, my first taste of philanthropy. It was very different from anything that would eventually involve the Sutton Trust. It was hands-off. But the way I saw it, it was a version of leverage. I put some money into something and it produced something far greater.

It also put a further thought in my mind. Maybe there were other things I could do with my money.

12

BACK TO SCHOOL (AND BACK TO COLLEGE)

The process by which the Sutton Company became the Sutton Trust was a gradual one. There was no thunderclap, no blinding flash of light. There was no lengthy internal debate at the end of which I went out onto a balcony and announced to the world: 'Right, that's it. Tomorrow, I embark on a heroic quest to become Britain's leading educational philanthropist – whether or not anybody can name another one.' The one concern gradually morphed into the other over a period of about a year. The work in education grew and began to dominate, and I eventually got out of leveraged buy-outs altogether. I was seeing results, and the results were so good and so satisfying that I kept on doing it.

However, beyond the nudge that the success of the Dunblane campaign had given me, there were two events that clearly set me on the philanthropic path I ended up taking. The first came one day in the mid-1990s when I was invited to visit my old school, Reigate Grammar. Have

I mentioned that I can still recite my Reigate Grammar School class list from 1959?

Addison, Avernell, Barton, Black ...

We did that already? OK, never mind.

The point is, I went back to Reigate, at the invitation of the head, getting on for 40 years after I had first walked through the gate. It was obviously a nostalgic moment. And in some ways, the place was exactly as I remembered it: the buildings were highly familiar; it still smelled the same. Yet clearly, in other respects, things had changed greatly while I had been living in the US and not really paying attention. On the plus side, T. W. H. Holland was no longer around as head, of course, and nobody seemed to be under threat from 'the swish'. And the swimming pool seemed to be heated at last. These 1990s pupils were living a charmed life, clearly.

There was one big difference, though: the school was now all fee-paying.

In my day, Reigate had been a state-funded independent school and free at the point of use. But, in common with nearly all other such schools, in 1976 it had its state funding withdrawn and was presented with the choice between merging with the comprehensive school system and becoming a fee-paying school. It did the latter.

When I was being shown around, I asked how much it was costing parents to send their children there. In today's money, it was about £6,000 per term – around £18,000 per year. That's a big sum of money for almost everybody. And imagine if you were trying to put two children through that school, or three. It was ironic to reflect that Reigate Grammar had been founded in 1675 as a free school for poor children. Now it was exclusively catering for the well-off.

And here was the part that bit deepest: I couldn't speak for everyone in my class, from Addison to Wright. But I was certain that I couldn't have gone there now. Neither, for that matter, could Peter Gershon. Neither of our families could have afforded to send us. So that was an impactful moment: to go back to your old school and find that children like the one that you had been were no longer acceptable there.

I was still mulling over all of that when Corpus Christi invited me to lunch. Why was I suddenly getting all these invitations to revisit my former educational haunts? What could explain my new-found popularity as a table-guest among schools and colleges? Might it have had something to do with the fact that I had made some money and might be in a position to give some of it away? I'll leave you to draw your own conclusions. All I'm saying is that Corpus extended the hand of friendship not long after Reigate had done so, and I went along.

The president of the college, and my host at this lunch, was Professor Keith Thomas, a top historian and, incidentally, a brilliant, dry-witted speaker whose talent in that area I could only envy. Keith had been given a knighthood in 1988. He was Welsh, from Wick in Glamorgan, and a grammar school boy – he had been to Barry County Grammar School. Talking to him, I was reminded that in my time at Corpus there had been a lot of Welsh kids who had come from working-class homes in the Valleys and had been to some good grammars. I was thinking particularly of my pal Laurence Eaves, but there had been several others in my year. I asked Keith if that was still the case.

'They don't really apply,' he said, 'and if they do, they're generally not at the level where we can take them.'

That seemed sad, and also a bit puzzling to me. Back at home, I did some research. The numbers of kids from state and state-funded independent schools achieving entry into Oxford had declined drastically from when I was there. In my time, these students had accounted for around two-thirds of the university's intake; now they were less than 50 per cent. That shouldn't be right, should it? Not given the overall proportion of state-educated kids to privately educated kids in the UK's population as a whole – 7 per cent private to 93 per cent state.

Now, obviously the decline was in part down to the closure of the grammar schools. But another path had also been blocked off for children from lower-income homes. In my day, the Direct Grant scheme and local authorities had ensured that over half the places at private day schools in any year were state-funded. But funding for Direct Grant schools had been abolished along with the grammars. The combined effect of those changes had radically altered the whole ethos. There were suddenly loads of schools in the system which used to be state-funded private schools and were now fee-paying, so only kids from wealthy backgrounds could afford to go. The comprehensive system, phased in by the Labour government from 1965 onwards, undeniably had its advantages, and was founded upon many plainly good intentions in relation to equality of opportunity. But we have never had a properly comprehensive system in this country. Money has continued to buy advantage, whether through independent school fees, tutoring kids for the 11-plus exam, or buying a house in a leafy catchment area. So, as it operated in practice, the comprehensive system was proving to have a fundamental downside, too: it was narrowing the opportunities for bright kids from low-income backgrounds. If you averaged out the figures, each of the country's 3,000 state secondary schools was managing to get a student into Oxbridge once every few years. In all fairness, how could you realistically expect Oxford and Cambridge to pay any kind of detailed attention to those schools, when the numbers of successful applicants they were seeing were so small? And more importantly, how could those schools devote time and resources to that area when their success rate at Oxbridge was so small? By contrast, there were now many rich and thriving independent schools out there, carefully geared up to getting kids into the top places. Those private schools were running like well-oiled machines and steering large numbers of applicants into Oxbridge every year – and not just into Oxbridge, as I realized when I examined the figures more closely, but into all the Russell Group universities (which is to say the collective, now 24 strong, of top British research universities).

I found all of this profoundly depressing. I was proud of my background and I knew how much I owed to state-funded education and the social mobility it clearly produced in a country in which a refugee's son from a council estate in Yorkshire could end up at Oxford. But what had happened to that social mobility since then? The machinery seemed to have seized up. Worse, it had gone into reverse.

Shouldn't something be done about that? I thought it should. And given that I suddenly seemed to have Oxford's ear, I decided to exploit that fact. Not long after the lunch at Corpus, I approached the admissions people at Oxford. At that meeting, I said, 'You've got a problem. Kids from state schools aren't getting in to your university, and fewer of them are bothering to apply.'

Their response was: 'It's not really our problem. If they don't apply, we can't admit them.'

My reply to that was: 'Well maybe you should do something to encourage them to apply.'

They didn't seem enthusiastic.

Nevertheless, I put to them an idea I had had. If schools weren't putting the idea of Oxbridge into their brightest kids' heads because the doors seemed firmly closed and they didn't consider it worth bothering, then maybe some kind of intervention needed to happen. What if the university were to invite along kids from schools that Oxford never heard from? You could gather up some bright pupils from places that had sent no or very few children to Oxford and you could bring them into the university for a week – during the summer holidays, say, when the colleges weren't busy. And during those days you would give those kids at least a taste of the place: what it felt like, how it worked, what it offered. It would be like a summer school, and maybe some of them would hate it and decide the place really wasn't for them. But maybe some of them would find it spoke to them in some way, and that little bit of exposure to life at Oxford would change their aspirational horizon and they would apply. And who knows? Maybe some of them would even get in, though of course that would be up to Oxford.

The Oxford admissions people still weren't enthusiastic.

Then I said, 'I'll pay for it.'

Suddenly they were enthusiastic.

So now I had a project: to design an effective summer school programme at Oxford for potential university students who might not otherwise have considered Oxford an option. The overarching purpose was clear: to demystify the place. We would set up some subject-specific lectures and some tutorials, so the kids could see how that worked. We would provide some mentoring from students already at Oxford, who would tell them about their experiences. We wanted it to be partly academic, but partly fun, too: it was the summer holidays, after all. So maybe we would take them out punting. And there should definitely be a practical administrative element: sessions on how the

Oxbridge admissions process works and how to apply.

Once we had a shape for the course, Oxford reached out to comprehensive schools around the country that weren't sending children to Oxbridge. We asked them to put forward bright kids who they thought might benefit from the kind of week we were offering (entirely free of charge). They needed to be plausible candidates in the school's opinion. Our criteria were that the kids should come from low-income backgrounds and from families with no tradition of sending children to university. We wanted these kids to be the first in their family to go.

The initial response was encouragingly positive. Heads of schools said they would give it a shot and eventually we ended up with a group of 64 kids drawn from across the UK.

I watched those kids arrive and check in and be issued with the keys to a typical undergraduate room and a timetable of activities. They were a pretty ragged band: trainers and T-shirts for the most part. Perhaps they didn't look like a typical Oxford cohort. If so, good. It meant we had got the right kids.

I couldn't remember ever feeling quite as nervous as I felt that first morning. I felt nervous for myself, because I wanted this thing to succeed very badly, and, as thoroughly as we had prepared, there still seemed to me to be any number of ways in which it could fall flat on its face. And I felt nervous for the kids, because I wanted this event to work for them and I didn't want to see bafflement or boredom or contempt or anything negative in their eyes. I wanted it to be revelatory – maybe even life-changing, if that wasn't too much to hope for.

So they did the lectures and the tutorials and went punting and to the cinema. I was there throughout, looking on from the sidelines, trying not to seem too anxious. It all seemed to go OK and the kids had seemed pretty positive about it, but who knew? The applications process would unfold over the autumn and winter. All I could do was wait and see.

Of our 64 kids, most eventually applied to Oxford, and a quarter ended up getting in. When news of those 16 acceptances came through the following January, it was the most amazing thing. These were bright kids who were set to pass under the radar as far as top-level university admissions were concerned, and certainly under the Oxbridge radar; and 16 of them ended up getting offers to go to Oxford as undergraduates. And the reason that they got accepted by the way, wasn't because they had attended a Sutton Trust summer school. The Sutton Trust summer school was merely the reason that they had applied. After that, they were in open competition with all the other applicants. So, the reason these kids got into Oxford was because they were good enough. That was the most deeply satisfying aspect of it to me. They were there because they belonged there.

So that was the outcome that really got me started and in effect sounded last orders for the Sutton Company and my time in leveraged buy-outs. That work was rewarding in its own way, but not like this. I realized that without spending a particularly large amount of money, I could make a big difference to people's lives. To put it in business terms: the leverage was huge. And clearly there was huge scope to expand this project.

With that first Oxford summer school under my belt, I decided to spread the message to Cambridge. Part of that process involved addressing a dinner one evening at Peterhouse, an old, mothy place that didn't seem to have changed all that much in the seven centuries since it was founded. (It's the oldest Cambridge college.) The ancient dining hall was lit entirely by candlelight – all very romantic, of course, though when the plates had been cleared and I stood up and removed from my inside pocket the notes I had prepared for my speech, I realized that, thanks to the gloom, I couldn't read a word of them. Nor had I thought to pack a torch.

It was a horrible feeling. Two hundred expectant faces peered up at me through the gloom. Fortunately, the vice-chancellor of Cambridge University was on hand. This was Alec Broers, later Lord Broers, a professor of electrical engineering who had worked for 19 years in the States for IBM, before returning to Cambridge as vice-chancellor, yet who wasn't above taking a candelabra off the table and holding it near me for a few minutes so that I could make my speech. And without setting fire to me, too. Very gracious of him.

After the dinner, the assembled high and mighty stood around chatting.

'This is a great initiative,' Alec said to me.

'I'm really glad you think so,' I replied.

'There's only one problem with it,' he went on. 'Oxford got there first.'

But Cambridge did come on board the following year, 1998. In fact, our Cambridge summer school grew over the years to the point where it is now our biggest – 600 students per year. Bristol and Nottingham came on board that year, too. They were all persuaded of the value of what we were offering, which was essentially some fresh thinking about the importance of outreach, a topic they had been ignoring. They could see the clear benefits of it – for the students, obviously, but also for themselves. None of these places wanted to be an elite mono-culture with next to no relation to the social mix of the country beyond its walls – the country into which most of its students would eventually emerge and go to work. Our summer schools could help universities tap into a pool of ultra-smart students that the system had closed off to them, and enable those institutions to reap the benefits in terms of their own diversity and dynamism.

Were there bumps along the way? Of course. There was the time we had an outbreak of norovirus at a summer school at the University of East Anglia in Norwich. Over those miserable five days, I would prefer to draw a veil, as well as a number of disinfectant-soaked cloths.

And then there was the slight wrinkle when I gave an interview about the Trust to the *Guardian* newspaper. I was discovering that my evolving position at the head of a new charitable body had a public element – something for which I hadn't really prepared. After all, talking to the national print media hadn't really been necessary when I was involved with building materials companies, and I would have avoided it like the plague in any case. So, as a neophyte, I sat down with a *Guardian* journalist and mentioned that Corpus hadn't taken any Welsh students in a while.

Now, my point was that Oxbridge had a systemic problem with state school children, of which the lack of plausible and successful candidates from working-class Welsh backgrounds was just one feature. But I didn't phrase it very carefully, so it came across that I was suggesting the college had some kind of problem with Welsh people. When this quote eventually appeared in print, Corpus, not unreasonably, took offence. The college said it would sue me if I didn't publicly retract, and things got a little ugly for a while. It felt odd, I must say, to have my alma mater threatening me with legal retribution, not least when the dean of that very college had once accompanied me to court in order to speak stoutly in defence of my good character. (I refer you, and the jury, to the nefarious tale of my freshers' week drunkenness recounted in Chapter 4.) Anyway, Corpus put some pressure on me, I eventually backed down and apologized, and the whole thing blew over with no lasting harm. Lesson learned about taking due care in newspaper interviews.

Otherwise, though, the scheme raced forwards very happily, expanding all the way. By 2006, 2,100 sixth-formers were applying for the 650 places we had on offer at summer schools at Oxford, Cambridge, Bristol, Nottingham and St Andrews. Of the 650 students who attended, half ended up applying to that particular university, and one in three got a place. Eventually we were able to use Sutton Trust summer school alumni as mentors, so the kids were getting it straight from the horse's mouth – hearing encouraging tales from people who had been to a summer school, applied to university, been accepted, graduated and gone on to find jobs. That made it all so much more real.

By 2019 we were receiving five applicants for every summer school place we could offer. More than 20,000 students had attended Sutton Trust summer schools and 62 per cent of those attendees had gone on to be accepted by a Russell Group university. In 2020, at the time of writing, we have 2,500 students attending summer schools at 13 top universities. Remember, these are kids from families with no history of university-going, and from schools with little history of inserting students into top-flight higher education. In that sense, they represent a vast infusion of fresh blood into the university system. And we have built a reputation among universities as an honest broker, supplying them with access to a stream of enormously capable students from overlooked and under-resourced places. We have also established ourselves with teachers, students and universities as an honest broker – simply wanting what is best for the kids.

The excitement and satisfaction that I drew from the success of this project were immense. OK, I probably got carried away and spent too much of my own money on it. I funded it for 15 years before I discovered, belatedly, that I didn't need to because we could raise that money, which we now do. My mistake. But who cares?

You would hear the stories, for example that of a boy called Luke Burton, the son of a self-employed mechanic living in Bristol. Neither of his parents had been to university and neither of them really expected Luke to think about it either. But his grandmother saw the Sutton Trust summer school notice in *The Sun* newspaper one day and tore it out and gave it to Luke. So he ended up spending a week at Oxford and getting a taste for it. And then he applied, and soon after that he was reading maths at Magdalen College.

Or there was Anu Damale, who went to the Cambridge Physics Summer School in 2014, became the first person from her state school in Southall to go to Durham University, read physics and went on to become a master's student in the Science Policy Research Unit.

Or there was Sam Turner from North Shields, whose mother's schooldays ended after O levels because her family couldn't afford the glasses she needed to read the blackboard, and who attended the Cambridge Summer School in 2008, read geography at Cambridge and went to work in the charity sector.

Or there was Emily Gotch, from a low-income rural family in the Cotswolds, who attended a summer school in 2013, read anthropology at UCL and went to work for Microsoft.

But I don't need to speak for these people. They speak for themselves far more eloquently than I ever could, and that's the whole point.*

So, the summer schools were up and running and getting results. The obvious next thought was: where else can we attack this problem? Where else can we remove the barriers keeping less privileged kids away from the best universities? How else can we oil up a process that seems to have rusted solid? Again, the numbers brought you up short. Our research showed six top private schools that were getting an amazing percentage of their sixth form into Oxbridge. The data also showed two state sixth form colleges rubbing shoulders with that elite group in terms of numbers, but with a lower hit rate, given their large size. It was staggering when you thought about it.

My notion was that we needed to tap into the independent schools in some way. Whatever else you might want to say about those places, when it came to getting kids into top universities, they were clearly the experts. What about tapping up those successful schools for what they knew and seeing if they would be prepared to share it? I talked to two independent school heads – at King Edward's School in Birmingham, and at Dulwich College in south London. These were former Direct Grant schools with experience,

* Some of the summer school alumni have contributed story blogs to our website. You can hear their voices loud and clear by visiting www. suttontrust.com.

not all that long ago, of taking kids from all backgrounds, not just wealthy ones. I said, 'You're very good at securing kids places at good universities. How about working with state schools in your area?' My idea was that these heads could work with the heads of comprehensives and offer to help their bright kids with tuition, with the university application process – in any way that was appropriate. Both ran with the idea, and I managed to get collaborative schemes up and running at both those schools.

Just as those two partnerships were going ahead and doing OK, I was introduced to Stephen Byers, who was Minister for Schools in Tony Blair's Labour government. Byers brought some scorn down on himself when, during a government numeracy drive, he was asked what 7 x 8 was and came up with the answer '54'. But hey, we all make mistakes.* And you take as you find. I had dinner with Byers at Mosimann's in Belgravia and he seemed smart enough to me. Labour had just got rid of the Assisted Places scheme, a Conservative policy dating back to 1980, which had been intended to fill, to a small extent, the gap

---

* Mathematicians broadly agree that 7 x 8 is 56. In a colourful political career, which all lay ahead of him at this point, Byers also found himself caught in a scandal when his political adviser, Jo Moore, sent him an email which alleged that, with the world necessarily distracted, September 11th 2001 would be 'a very good day to get out anything we want to bury'. I guess, in her defence, she wasn't wrong. Byers knew still further indignity when a Merseyside councillor recalled joining him for a drink in his hotel room during the Labour party conference and finding him naked but for a pair of black socks. It was the black socks that really seemed to upset people.

left by the Direct Grant scheme, but which had been flawed in both concept and implementation, and the government was now looking for some way of dealing with the independent education sector. Byers asked me if I would co-fund one year of partnerships between independent and state schools, along the lines of the schemes we had developed with Dulwich College and King Edward's. I put up a few hundred grand for a few years and we got a big scheme going, Independent/State School Partnerships (ISSPs), which eventually had a £2 million per year budget. That was a big success. By 2017, it was estimated that 175,000 state school pupils were benefitting from partnership initiatives involving private schools. Lord Nash, the Parliamentary Under-Secretary of State for Schools, who had been my contemporary at Corpus, said, 'ISSPs have been a hugely successful – and durable – initiative which has had a real impact on the quality of learning in partner schools.' Nowadays, practically all independent schools have partnerships of some kind with state schools. It has become embedded in the system.

By now I was thinking, 'This is really quite exciting, running with these guys.'

The next key person I met was David Blunkett, the Secretary of State for Education. It was the first time I had a meeting with a member of the Cabinet. I assumed it would just be me and Blunkett, having a quick head-to-head chat. But no. I walked into the room and I looked around and there seemed to be a whole football team in there, with Blunkett somewhere in the middle of it. I don't know where they all came from: assistants, advisers, civil servants ... I thought to myself: 'OK, so this is the way government works: everybody has to be there.'

But I liked and admired Blunkett. I would rank him as one of the most impressive politicians I ever met. I invited him to the summer schools. He came to one in Oxford, and he really got it – to the point, in fact, where he adopted it. Getting kids to go to university was one of the Labour government's key areas of interest. They took our summer schools programme model, which was designed for 17-year-olds, and applied it to 16-year-olds, pre-GCSE, as part of a drive to persuade more children to stay on for A levels.

After I had met Blunkett, Michael Wills, MP for Swindon North (now Lord Wills), arranged for me to get together with Gordon Brown, who would go on to take the top job at Number 10, but who was then the Chancellor of the Exchequer. I went along to the Treasury and was shown into a vast conference room with an enormous table. I expected to be chaperoned by Michael Wills, but he was late for some reason, and would eventually burst in, hot and breathless, about half an hour later. So it was me and Gordon at that giant table, just the two of us. We seemed to understand each other well.

Not long after this, the phone rang at home and Karen answered it. 'It's someone called Gordon,' she said, passing the phone over. The Chancellor wanted to get some advice from me on what became known as 'the Laura Spence affair'. Spence was a state school student from Whitley Bay who got into the newspapers in 2000 when Magdalen

College, Oxford, rejected her application to study medicine, despite the fact that she had ten A* GCSEs and was predicted to get (and, indeed, eventually did get) top grades in four A level subjects. Brown mentioned her case in a speech at a Trades Union Congress, calling it 'an absolute scandal' and suggesting that she had been the victim of the 'old establishment interview system'. The controversy generated by Spence's story, and by Brown's very public (and, some insisted, uncalled-for) intervention, helped take the debate about access to higher education into the mainstream.*

I met Gordon again just before he became Prime Minister and we discussed the fact that since 1940 every English Prime Minister who had been to university (which was all bar three) had gone to Oxford, so he would be breaking the mould. And that's just what he did. When he was PM, he spoke at the Sutton Trust's 10th anniversary celebration at the Banqueting House on Whitehall. He spoke authoritatively and engagingly about the Trust, completely without notes. There were lots of ministers there who said it was one of the best speeches he'd ever given.

Because I felt I needed a flagship vehicle for this new work, I set up the Sutton Trust, which was basically a matter of taking the Sutton Company name and registering it as a charity. I gave up the office in Belgravia that I had taken for the Sutton Company's UK operations and rented

* Spence was accepted by Harvard and later studied at Cambridge.

a space in Wimbledon, near where I lived. Perhaps it wasn't as fancy, but it was still a proper office – somewhere you wouldn't mind bringing people for a meeting. I might have been moving into philanthropy, but as far as I was concerned, the same rules applied: if you wanted people to think you were a solid operation, you needed to look like a solid operation.

I had with me Anna Fellows, my assistant, who had been with the Sutton Company for ten years, but who now loyally and unflinchingly transitioned into guiding me every step of the way while I built a charitable trust. Anna is one of the major reasons for my success. When I got my knighthood, I said I thought it ought to have been shared between us. I also had Laura Barbour on board as the Trust's administrator. Again, the great wisdom holds true: get the very best people around you. Anna, Laura – these were the very best people, without whom the Trust would never have got off the ground. Laura had been to Wycombe Abbey in Buckinghamshire and I used to tease her that she was 'proper posh' and ask her what she was doing with us. She was the organizational dynamo who gave the Trust shape in those early days, and she is still with us.

I was interested in what the top American universities were doing in terms of outreach and admissions. I knew there would be plenty I could learn from them. So Laura and I set off on a fact-finding trip, driving through New England, where many of the best US universities were clustered, and getting as much information as we could about these places and the way they behaved. We started out in

Boston, at MIT and Harvard, and then drove down to Brown on Rhode Island, and then Yale, Princeton, Columbia and the University of Pennsylvania. It was fall, when the leaves do their famous thing in that part of the world, so the trip was no hardship. The scenery was breathtaking.

I had an entry to these top colleges because, to put it bluntly, I had made a lot of money. As I had already experienced at Corpus Christi, nobody opens the doors to academe quite as easily as a potential benefactor. In my position, and with what I was trying to achieve, not to exploit that fact would have been crazy.

That said, in one respect it wouldn't have mattered who I was. An instantly visible contrast between the American and British way of doing things was in the attitude universities had to open days. At Harvard, I learned that you could show up at 10 a.m. as a punter, straight off the street, without an appointment, any day of the week, and an admissions officer would talk to you about the entry process and students would show you around some of the buildings and chat to you about how they found life there. Meanwhile the university carried on going about its business in front of your eyes. This was true of all the universities we visited.

By contrast, Oxford was holding three open days a year, and Cambridge was holding two. The demand was massive, and on each of those occasions the university was effectively shut down. When you got there, it was like a railway station at rush hour, with hundreds of people milling around. I'm not sure what the value was. In those circumstances, you're not experiencing the university as it is; you're experiencing the university as it is when it's holding an open day.

When I talked to the Admissions Director at Harvard she invited me to come back during admissions season, and sit in on an admissions committee meeting. It turned out to be a pivotal experience – one that shaped my thinking. That day, the committee was sitting around a huge table looking at applications from high school students from southern California, going over the paperwork and trying to decide which kids to offer places to. In among the batch were an awful lot of clearly super-smart kids, many with perfect SATs, playing the piano and the violin virtually to concert standard, and so on. But there was also an application from a black girl from the Watts district of Los Angeles, who had less than perfect SATs and who gave no indication of having spent much time around pianos and violins. Yet by the end of the meeting, the black girl was in, and a number of kids with perfect SATs and musical gifts were not.

I went up to the chair of the meeting afterwards and asked her about it: how had this particular kid, seemingly a long way down the ladder, come to prevail over so many practically faultless applicants?

The chair smiled and said, 'We did a lot of research on her. We think she's got huge potential. She's the kind of person who could be the mayor of a major city one day, or senior partner in a law firm. And by the way, we're in the value-added business.'

That phrase leapt out at me: 'the value-added business'. It wasn't the kind of thing that you would have heard Oxbridge admissions people say: the focus there was on getting the folk who were going to get the best degrees. They wouldn't have talked in those terms, just as they wouldn't have considered the notion of balancing the class. Yet those words seemed to me to be revelatory and to cut through to an important truth about top-flight education and what it ought to be aiming to do. Say an Oxbridge college takes someone from, for example, Eton. The chances are the college is not going to be adding much value. More than likely, it will just be giving a further polish to something that was probably already quite shiny to begin with. The greater ambition for an educational institution, surely, is to add value in substantial measures – to make the most significant difference that it can in each individual case. Universities should, indeed, be in the value-added business. The phrase came away with me from that Harvard meeting and stuck. It became the key question to ask when assessing projects with the Sutton Trust. How much value are we adding when we do this? How can we maximize the added value? It's a touchstone.

After that fact-finding trip, I got excited about the possibility of getting bright, less privileged British kids into American universities. Britain was already sending students to America for degree education, but it was almost invariably kids from private schools. State schools didn't seem to be considering it. Yet means-tested grants were available. That girl from Watts whose admission review I witnessed would be going to Harvard on a 'full ride' – everything paid for. Children from less privileged backgrounds weren't excluded from applying to these places, they just didn't seem to realize they had the opportunity.

I had the idea of duplicating the Sutton Trust's British summer schools in America – taking groups of less privileged kids from the UK and giving them a taste of life at top American colleges, such as Yale and Harvard and MIT, just to see if it chimed with any of them. We had a meeting with people from the Fulbright Commission, which was best known for organizing post-graduate student exchanges between the US and Britain. I agreed to stump up the cash and they agreed to help us develop a summer programme in which we would fly over a group of sixth-form kids and show them around some of the top places. The same criteria that we used for the British summer schools would apply here: the kids had to come from low-income backgrounds, from families with no history of university attendance and had to be genuine candidates.

We canvassed British state schools again, asking them to put forward bright pupils who might be contenders. We ended up with 64 kids on the pilot, which we designed to mirror the numbers on the first Oxford summer school. It made for a hectic scene at Heathrow Terminal 3. Everybody was issued with a bright yellow Sutton Trust backpack so that we didn't lose anyone. Some of these kids had never been on a plane before, let alone the US. Among them was a home-schooled girl from Newlyn in Cornwall, an Academy school boy from Derby, Chloë from Essex, whose mother was a cleaner, a kid from a Dagenham housing estate, a half-Jamaican, half-Irish Olympic platinum sports ambassador from Tottenham, and Stephanie from the Wirral, whose parents couldn't afford music lessons, so she had taught herself to play the oboe by watching videos on YouTube.

On the first morning, I gave an introductory talk in the hall at Yale. I explained that, at an American university, on a four-year course, you would spend the first year doing a variety of things before you specialized, unlike the British system, which insists on specialization straight away. I said to them, 'I've brought you here because Britain is just a small island off the coast of Europe, while America is a vast and exciting place, full of possibility. Ninety-three per cent of British kids are educated in state schools and hardly any of them are taking advantage of the opportunities on offer in the US. I want that to change.'*

After my speech, we had a Q&A and a hand went up.

'You went to Oxford,' one of the students said. 'Would you rather have gone to Yale?'

'Yes, I would,' I replied without hesitation, extremely mindful of where I was.

The group then went off to take part in taster seminars on such subjects as medicine, galaxies and universes, the outlaw in film, and cooking and culture. Again, the event

---

* Later, when I was at Harvard, an admissions tutor said, 'Here you'll learn a little bit about a lot of things, and a lot about a little.' That focus on breadth has always seemed a good approach to me.

seemed to pass off well, but there was another agonizing wait before we could see whether it had paid off or not.

It certainly had. Lucinda Denney from Blackpool Sixth-Form College won a four-year scholarship to Yale. Ben Devanay, who lived with his aunt and uncle in Wolverhampton and went to a comprehensive there, won a full scholarship to a top university. Twenty-one kids from that initial group of 64 ended up getting into the best US universities on full rides. It was a staggering outcome.

That was the beginning of the Sutton Trust US Programme, which runs every year. We have built a relationship with every top US university, to go with the relationships we have with every top UK university. In 2019 we flew out 200 students, our largest ever contingent, on summer school programmes to MIT, Yale, Princeton and Duke in North Carolina. At the time of writing, the Trust has completely transformed the lives of 412 kids by carefully helping them find, apply for and secure places at over 70 top American universities. To date, 28 have been accepted at Princeton, 22 at Yale and 19 at Harvard. But no matter where they go, they prosper there. I get emails from the likes of Harvard and MIT, saying how thrilled they are with these students. I'm not blind to some of the unsavoury practices that have occasionally sullied the reputation of the US university admissions system, most notoriously the buying of favour brought to light in the 2019 college admissions bribery scandal. But as the Trust has encountered, the US system's determination to reward excellence and potential ahead of economic status has been outstandingly dynamic and refreshing and serves as a shining example to other countries.

The US colleges that we deal with have shown themselves willing to pay up to $300,000 to take a kid from Britain who may have got lower exam results than kids on the college's doorstep. Nobody, to my knowledge, in the UK does that. Practically all the foreign students who go to UK universities are, of necessity, rich kids who pay double – or certainly well-supported kids. It's not entirely helpful in terms of the social mix.

So why are these US colleges taking low-income British kids who don't have the same test scores as kids they're turning away? For three reasons. First, because those kids have demonstrated, through aptitude and potential, that they belong there. Second, because these universities accept that you learn as much if not more from your fellow students than you do from professors and tutors, so a diverse group is crucial.

And third, because those elite US colleges are in the value-added business, as top educational facilities ought to be.

13

OPEN ACCESS

Every country has problems with its schools, but Britain has a unique set of them. It has a rigid division between the privately funded and the state-funded sectors and a yawning gap in achievement between them – the biggest of any advanced country. The differences in facilities, teacher qualifications, teacher–pupil ratios and performance are vast. And the highest-performing schools are closed to the vast majority, who can't afford the fees. The UK hosts a two-nation education system – a system of educational apartheid, a phrase I didn't coin but certainly found myself using a lot as I worked to carry the Sutton Trust forward.

The educational advantages enjoyed by privileged families in Britain are not seen to the same extent anywhere else in the developed world. It's a situation that baffles foreign observers, and it was a situation that baffled a returning ex-pat like me.

As I quickly discovered, to stumble into this area is to land up in the middle of one of Britain's most furious ideological battlegrounds. Yet it's a battleground on which the same battle seems to get fought over and over again, by the same people, using the same weapons, with no effect ultimately, and with no outcome other than to reinforce the status quo. For some, the only solution is the extreme one: to abolish the private sector and implement a stand-alone comprehensive system. But there are complex issues around freedom and rights. If you banned private education, would you also have to ban home-schooling? What would you do about people who were in the comprehensive system yet who chose to buy their kids extra tuition at home? Would that have to be illegal too? The most likely outcome of a bid to terminate them would be years of legal wrangling, at the end of which nothing much would have changed except that a few lawyers would have got even richer than they already were.

Also, those schools are really good. At 15, British private school kids top global lists in terms of attainment. In that sense it seemed ridiculous to start talking about bulldozing them. Surely it would be better to find a different way to use what they have – to open them up.

When the Trust began to address this area, I was temperamentally inclined to go about things the way I had always done – pragmatically. I was trying to develop an organization that could make practical, programmatic interventions that resulted in actual change. I wasn't setting up an ideological 'think-tank' – a term I dislike, by the way. If I'm going to be in charge of a tank, I'd like it to do something more than think. If the Sutton Trust was going to be any kind of tank, I wanted it to be a do-tank.

So, what were the realities here, and what could we do about them? Should private schools be abolished and the system switched by mandate to fully comprehensive with no opt-outs? You could argue that this is not a bad idea. It's what Finland did and they've arguably got the best education system in Europe. But was it going to happen? Almost certainly not – and definitely not in my lifetime. So why not work with what was there? Open the independent schools up. Democratize them. Spread their benefits across the population more widely. That seemed to be a project to which the Trust could profitably apply itself.

Education secretaries down the years had said they wanted to see a widening of the collaboration between the state sector and the independent sector. But none of them had pushed it anywhere near as far as I thought it could be pushed. The Trust thought about this long and hard, and the vision we came up with for that wider collaboration was a scheme we called 'Open Access'. It was an idea that had first been mooted by George Walden, a former Conservative Minister for Higher Education and a passionate believer in providing paths for bright poorer kids. In collaboration with the Girls' Day School Trust (GDST), a 25-strong union of UK independent schools whose chief executive, Michael Oakley, was a formative force behind this project, we trialled Open Access over a seven-year period from 2000 at Belvedere Girls' School in Liverpool. It was the most ambitious project the Trust had attempted, and I don't think it's any kind of exaggeration to say that for me, personally, it became a mission, one that I am still driving away at.

Essentially we were taking our work on Independent/State School Partnerships ten steps further. That work had usefully blurred the divide between state and private, but it hadn't overcome it. The basic question we now asked ourselves was: what if the best-performing UK independent day schools were open to all? What if you could unlock their doors to *all* the top talents, not just the comfortably-off top talents, and have a system in which entry was on merit alone, entirely independent of the ability to pay? Fees would be charged on a sliding scale, adjusted according to means, with the richest continuing to pay full fees and shading off to the poorest, who would pay nothing. In effect, it was the 'needs-blind admissions' scheme adopted by top American universities, although in that case the funding to make up the inevitable shortfall comes from the universities' own endowments, which don't exist in this country to anything like the same degree. (Oxford and Cambridge, which have by far the largest endowments in the UK, would only rank in the high teens on the US list, where Harvard leads the pack with a staggering $41 billion.) In our version of this scheme, we would look to the government to pick up the tab.

Now, when I was initially trying to convince people of this idea, this was the point at which they would start twitching a bit. State funding? For private schools? Surely no sensible government would want to be seen to be openly funding the independent sector ...

Probably not. But we had done the sums. In terms of cost per place, Open Access would actually be a better deal for the Treasury than the state education that they were funding already. At the point at which we did the modelling for our Belvedere project, the average annual cost to the government of a place for a pupil at a comprehensive was £4,300. At Belvedere, the cost of the supplementary funding – to be covered during the pilot by the Trust and the Girls' Day School Trust – worked out at £3,500 per place. So it was actually going to be cheaper, from the government's point of view, for a child to be in an Open Access school than in a state school – and you could immediately banish the objection that the Treasury was lavishing money on independents while neglecting state schools.

I wasn't thinking of Open Access as a substitute for the Assisted Places scheme of the 1980s, which had a lot of faults and saw a few 'poor scholars' parachuted into schools for the well-off, leaving the overall social mix unchanged – and frequently leaving those 'poor scholars' socially marooned. Because, let's face it, if you drop some poor kid into an elite private school, what are you actually achieving in terms of mixing up the prevailing culture?

Nor did I want Open Access to be confused in any way with the bursary schemes that independent schools often use as fig leaves in this area, but that sometimes look more like creative accounting than socially minded outreach. When a private school tells you that 30 per cent of its kids are receiving funding, always have your bullshit monitor close at hand. Schools use bursaries to subsidize fees for the children of teachers at the school, and to fund existing pupils whose parents get into difficulties (job loss, divorce). That's not exactly opening a school up. In fact just 1 per cent of kids in independent schools have all their fees met. So whatever the good intentions – and there undoubtedly are some – I'll never believe that bursaries are going to be the solution for bringing independent schools within reach for ordinary families.

Under the terms of Open Access, you wouldn't be expanding academic selection, which a lot of people have a problem with; you would be democratizing an area of selection that already exists. But now 100 per cent of the places in any year's intake would be awarded on merit, and that would radically and importantly change the social mix of the schools. These would no longer be exclusive institutions with a few places reserved for 'the deserving poor', but schools where everyone would be on an equal footing. It was easy to see how opening up independent schools would give pupils across the social spectrum access to the best-qualified teachers (our research had already revealed that these teachers were heavily concentrated in the independent sector). And in turn you would be starting to combat the snobbery, nepotism and envy that plague UK education.

The plan seemed completely convincing to me. It also seemed to convince the people I spoke to about it in government and in the independent sector. Or, at least, they did a lot of appreciative nodding while they listened to me. But getting people to commit to putting Open Access in place

... that was clearly going to be harder. It became obvious that the strongest pitch we could make on behalf of this approach was not just to talk to people about how it would work, but to demonstrate unequivocally that it did. And that was what led us to get together with the Girls' Day School Trust and organize the seven-year trial at Belvedere Girls' School.

Belvedere was the perfect school for our purposes. It was a high-performing independent school based in Toxteth, a poor and largely unregenerated inner-city district of Liverpool, attended by significant numbers of fee-paying children from all over Merseyside, but by far fewer children from its own immediate catchment area. It also had a head, Gill Richards, and a board of governors who were bold enough to embrace a fresh approach, and that, of course, was key. It was clear to us that if Open Access were to gain any kind of traction, it would need to be voluntary on the school's part in every case. It was also reassuring to be partnering with the Girls' Day School Trust, which had been a key player in the Direct Grant scheme and could bring a vast amount of expertise to the table. Nevertheless, it goes without saying that you don't casually enter into an experiment in which a bunch of kids' educations are at stake – from Year 7 through to the sixth form. There were plenty of occasions in the planning stages when I would catch myself thinking, 'This is pretty momentous. Are we sure?'

One of the first critical steps was to appoint an outreach officer to go into Liverpool's state primary schools and talk about the Belvedere pilot in the hope of dispelling any suspicion and uncertainty about it – and she, encouragingly, reported very little initial resistance in principle to the notion from state teachers, whose support we would need in putting their talented kids forward.

Meanwhile a whole new and more wide-ranging admissions procedure had to be drawn up to level the playing field between the sectors and remove the natural advantage that prep schools offered. Prep school kids were up on things because they had been given the opportunity to be up on them. Would the state school kids have been up on them too, if they had been given the chance? We wanted a level playing field on which we could fairly evaluate the relative potential of these kids – the likelihood that they would flourish in the Belvedere environment. Verbal and non-verbal reasoning tests were introduced alongside existing tests in English and maths and, crucially, we took detailed references from the pupils' primary schools. Gill, the head, then interviewed all the potential candidates.

At this point, we had no idea whether kids from the upper income bracket would dominate the intake. In 1999, a quarter of Belvedere's pupils had been receiving some kind of assistance with fees, mostly as surviving beneficiaries of the now terminated Assisted Places scheme. Three-quarters of the cohort were paying full fare. If our first round of needs-blind admissions returned a cohort on exactly the same proportions, we were going to end up feeling pretty flat – perhaps even a little foolish. We could only advertise our new opportunity as widely as possible and then wait with fingers crossed to see if the statistics changed.

The first hopeful sign in that initial year was the number of applications that came in. There were 69 places available, and 367 kids applied for them – two and a half times the number of pupils who had applied to Belvedere the previous year. That seemed promising.

The second encouraging sign was where those applications had come from. Twenty-five applicants were from Belvedere's own independent primary school, and a further 23 were from other independent schools. But the other 319 were from state schools on Merseyside. Already we could see that we were going to end up with a cohort that more closely represented the local population than had typically been the case.

As it turned out, the social mix in that first year under Open Access was pretty much the best we could have hoped for. In our first cohort at Belvedere, 30 per cent of the pupils were eligible for full funding, 40 per cent qualified for partial funding and the rest paid full fees. We had a mix of parents that ran from barristers to bartenders. With that 30–40–30 split in a school, you've certainly got a great social mix, and one that was different from any that Belvedere had been attracting when it was operating as a fully independent school. But now we would see if that year-group worked out in practice.

In September 2000, that group turned up for their first day of term. I was there to see them arrive and assemble in the hall for the first time – a big bundle of excitement and nervous energy. The pupils, I mean, though I was pretty much the same. Watching the first Sutton Trust summer school group show up in Oxford had been something, but this was on another level. I still choke up when I think about it now. Sixty-nine girls came into that hall, and 49 of them were there because of what we had done. Forty-nine of those girls were bright kids whose parents wouldn't have considered applying to a school like Belvedere a year before. Yet who would have known? That was the wonderful thing. The kids were all in uniform, and you couldn't pick them apart. They were just an energetic bunch of bright schoolchildren who belonged exactly where they were standing. That was my overriding feeling that morning, seeing those kids. 'This is your right,' I thought. 'It is your right to come to this school.' Those kids were there because they were clever enough to be there, and if they were clever enough to be there, then this was where they belonged.

'Even in its first year, the scheme can be counted a success.' That was the verdict of the independent annual assessment commissioned from Professor Alan Smithers from the Centre of Education and Employment Research at the University of Liverpool, which had looked in particular at the effect Open Access was having on entry to Belvedere in terms of ability and background. What was going on at the school was getting extremely positive reviews in the local press, too, where the change of status was celebrated as progressive. Given the choice between an old-fashioned independent school and a school that was an extension of choice for all, people's instinctive qualms about selection seemed to recede. And you only had to talk to the students, the teachers and the parents to know that Belvedere was functioning socially, with girls from diverse backgrounds working happily together and forging lasting friendships – in other words, where girls were getting the opportunity that I had been given, 45 years earlier, before the system froze and the doors closed on people like me.

By year three of the pilot we had applications from 129 state schools. Thirty per cent of those for whom the father's occupational status was available were from manual labour or unemployed backgrounds. That year 29 girls from the two poorest postcodes got places, and six girls were accepted from Liverpool's inner city. Across the first five years of the pilot, the number of girls at the school eligible for free school meals was 32.8 per cent, more than double the national average. However, people who could afford to pay full fees continued to do so, even when 30 per cent of the girls were going for free. If the school was good enough, people seemed happy to carry on paying.

Naturally, all this was costing me – about £1 million a year at the peak, in fact. (The Girls' Day School Trust was matching that.) But if entry based on merit had simply produced a cohort which was 100 per cent drawn from affluent, full fee-paying families, and all supplementary funding had been unnecessary, then the scheme would clearly have fallen on its face. So, to that extent, I was happy to foot the bill, even though the bill was rising with each passing year. That wasn't something I had ever felt about a bill before.

And I was especially happy when, after five years of Open Access, Belvedere reported its best ever GCSE results. In 2005, 99 per cent of its students achieved A–C grades at GCSE level. In the league tables, it was the best school on Merseyside and in the top 50 schools nationally. Of our first-year intake, only four had left the school (all of them fully fee-paying). All of the remaining girls were planning to go on to university. Ten were aiming to do medicine and nine were hoping to study law.

When the trial period ended, there were mixed feelings. On the one hand, Open Access had clearly been a resounding success. At the same time, it had been hard to resist the hope (always optimistic) that during the pilot, the government would be so persuaded by what we doing that they would jump on board, implement the scheme and enable Belvedere to sail on as Britain's pioneering Open Access school, with a fleet of eager early-adopters in its wake. Alas, the government continued to look on approvingly – and do nothing.

At the end of the trial, Belvedere had to look to its future. It considered reverting to fully independent status and decided instead to become an all-ability state-funded Academy school, the Belvedere Academy.

Still, the experiment had exceeded all our expectations. We had demonstrated what we had set out to show: that it was possible to bridge the country's educational divide while maintaining the highest academic standards, and to do so cost-effectively. We had showed conclusively that needs-blind entry to the top independent schools was good for those schools, good for the pupils – and, in the long term, surely, good for the country.

The concept remains alive. In September 2012, the heads of City of London, the Grammar School at Leeds, James Allen's Girls' School, The Godolphin and Latymer School, Dulwich College, the Royal Grammar School, Newcastle, and a total of 90 independent school heads all put their names to a letter indicating their willingness to admit pupils on merit alone, irrespective of whether their families could afford the fees. They all stated that they 'fully support the introduction of a state-funded Open Access scheme, as pioneered by the Sutton Trust'.

At that point, I had a private meeting with Michael Gove, who was the Education Secretary, and suggested that I organize a meeting for him with some of these heads so that he could hear from them the case for Open Access. Gove agreed to attend a get-together in the Department of Education and I went away to put the word out to the school heads. Sixty heads got back to say they would love to come. Realizing that this would cause a bit of a crush in the Department, I hired Church House directly opposite. I then called Gove to tell him that our meeting had got a little bigger. 'No problem,' he said.

But first thing the following morning, I got a call from his secretary. No way was Gove going to meet 60 school heads … 'He's only prepared to meet 12,' she said. So I scaled it down to a dozen, disappointing 48 eager attendees, and the meeting went ahead. Sadly, though, Gove got into what I call his 'Oxford Union debating mode' and the conversation didn't really go forward. The government still wouldn't come on board with Open Access.

We battle on regardless. Every time the Education Minister changes, every time the government changes, we take up the cudgels again, ready to play the long game if we have to. Around 2006 I met the Conservatives' new Shadow Minister for Higher Education, a charming chap with tousled blond hair called Boris Johnson. A little later, I found myself sharing a platform at an event in London with him. We left the building together and I watched him unchain his pushbike from a railing and pedal off into the night. 'Ah,' I thought to myself, 'those low-ranking politicians.' Fourteen years later, in 2020, that bloke on the pushbike was Prime Minister and I was writing to him at 10 Downing Street on the same theme.

But now I could tell him, and also Dominic Raab, the new Foreign Secretary, that we had garnered support for Open Access from 90 independent schools. Ten of those schools, including Westminster, St Paul's and Manchester Grammar, have declared themselves ready to participate in a ten-school trial to trailblaze the scheme, if the government subsidises the trial. If 100 schools were to go Open Access, we calculate that when the scheme is in a steady state it would enable 50,000 children whose parents couldn't afford private school fees to be privately educated. It would offer private schools a way to remain relevant, to contribute, and possibly even to win friends and supporters, which they have sorely lacked outside their own social niche these past decades. And it would turbocharge social mobility by taking children from lower-income backgrounds and giving them an education to match any in the world.

The apartheid mentality in the UK's education system does the country few favours. Supporting Open Access would be the simplest policy step a government could take to bridge the divide between the state and independent sectors and to boost social mobility at the top of society. We've already proved it works. So what are these people waiting for?

14

SOCIALLY MOBILE

As things gathered pace, the Trust outgrew its Wimbledon office. Tessa Stone joined us as my second in command. A Cambridge academic and former admissions tutor at Newnham College, she favoured a long, thick woollen coat which I presume would once have protected her from the driving winds that blow into the Cambridge fens direct from Russia, though south-west London was, in truth, a little more balmy. Anyway, Tessa stayed for six years, was a brilliant CEO and expertly built up a team which would become the backbone of the Trust. When that team numbered ten full-time staff, we moved to a bigger place in Putney. Then we outgrew the Putney office, too, and we moved to offices on the ninth floor of Millbank Tower, just along from the Tate Gallery on the north bank of the Thames, where we could more comfortably fit a staff that would grow to 30. This new home had views and light. And it had the convenience of being close to the hub of things at Westminster, where we were increasingly needed.

By then the Trust had long ceased to be some kind of side-line for me. This was work, and I went at it the way I had always worked, getting into the office at 6.45 in the morning before anyone else was there and very often leaving late.

We had seen how we could have an impact through programmes – the summer schools, the Belvedere pilot. Now, to increase our influence with policy-makers, we were ramping up our research. We realized that by writing or commissioning in-depth research papers which were eye-catching and challenging, we could establish the problems that concerned us, get a public conversation going and shift the debate into places where politicians couldn't ignore it.

In August 2004, we made our first big waves with a report we called 'The Missing 3,000'. It was based on analysis that we did which disclosed the alarming, possibly even scandalous, under-representation of state school pupils at the UK's leading universities. What we worked out was that every year about 3,000 students – 10 per cent of the total – from state schools and sixth-form colleges were not joining the 30,000 people admitted to the dozen leading universities, despite having gained grades as good as, or even better than, the grades gained by kids from independent schools. In other words, there were 3,000 independent school pupils going to the top universities each year who wouldn't have been there if higher-achieving state pupils had taken up their fair share of the places.*

---

* 'The Missing 3,000: State school students under-represented at leading universities', The Sutton Trust, August 2004.

Where were these missing 3,000 ending up? Many of them were going to new universities – the ones established after the 1992 Further and Higher Education Act – and, of course, that was fine. Many of those places were great and no doubt many of those kids were going on to do good things. Yet they were capable – and, in some cases, more than capable – of being at the leading institutions. So why weren't they there?

It was clear that many weren't even applying because they felt discouraged from doing so, or they lacked confidence. There also seemed to be a reluctance in state school pupils to pick a university far from home – a reluctance which independent school pupils didn't share. That, too, seemed connected to a certain kind of cultural confidence – and also, clearly, to financial wherewithal. But the broader point was that universities at this time had been encouraged, and funded, by the government to improve access, and the figures didn't suggest it was happening.

That 'Missing 3,000' report got a lot of media coverage. People seemed to fasten on to the story it told of lost talent – kids falling through the cracks, year after year. It was an education story, clearly, but at the same time it was a story about social mobility and the barriers impeding it. And social mobility was clearly an area where the Trust could and should be having an impact. When unfairness in education was allowed to exist, social mobility clearly suffered. It followed that if you were agitating for the removal of unfairness in the education system, you were agitating for social mobility.

Running with this thought, the Trust commissioned a report from the Centre for Economic Performance at the London School of Economics which sought to find out what had happened to social mobility in the UK over time and how the UK compared with other developed countries. The research was led by Stephen Machin, who is now head of the Centre. Its reports showed that those born in the 1950s had more chance of moving up the social ladder than those born in the 1970s – i.e. social mobility had declined. Furthermore, along with the US, the UK appeared to have the lowest level of social mobility of any developed country for which data was available.* Opportunity was no longer expanding, it was shrinking, and people down at the bottom end were increasingly getting marooned there.

I thought about the path my father had taken: a refugee from Vienna who had arrived in the UK with nothing more than a suitcase of clothes and a smattering of English and had ended up in an executive white-collar job and living in

---

* Jo Blanden, Paul Gregg and Stephen Machin, 'Intergenerational Mobility in Europe and North America', The Centre for Economic Performance in collaboration with the Sutton Trust, April 2005. And Jo Blanden and Stephen Machin, 'Recent Chances in Intergenerational Mobility in the UK', The Sutton Trust, December 2007. This problem has not gone away. Indeed, by some measures, it has worsened. In 2020, our research demonstrated that the probability of people in professional and managerial jobs having been from low- and moderate-income backgrounds had badly declined over time – from 20 per cent for those born in 1955–1961 to just 12 per cent for those born in 1975–1981. In other words, opportunities had almost halved. ('Elites in the UK: Pulling Away? Social mobility, geographic mobility and elite occupations', The Sutton Trust, January 2020.)

one of the smartest parts of Cheltenham. I thought about my own path, from a Yorkshire council estate to Oxford, and from Oxford to successful entrepreneur and philanthropist. What were the odds now for people trying to do the equivalent of what my father had done and what I had done? The Britain of my childhood had seemed a place of possibility where, with a fair wind and bit of good fortune, you could spring up from modest origins. But somewhere along the way that had changed. In the UK of the twenty-first century, you needed to be born at top of the social ladder, because your chances of finding any rungs lower down and clambering up were getting slimmer and slimmer. This surely was a systemic crisis which a body like the Sutton Trust should be creatively highlighting and working to change.

'It's simple,' said Rupert Murdoch. 'All you have to do is abolish Eton.'

We were sitting around a table in the media mogul's apartment in St James's in London. I had been invited to a small dinner organized by Rebekah Brooks, the chief executive of what was then News International, where the other guests included Lord Adonis, the Labour peer and Joel Klein, the former Chancellor of the New York City Department of Education (a huge role, overseeing 1,600 public schools) and then a legal adviser to News International. I had asked Murdoch what he thought could be done about social mobility and its decline in the UK, prompting him, perhaps not untypically, to propose that ground-zero solution. Well, maybe he had a point. But the

Sutton Trust preferred to take a more diplomatic approach: strategic research.*

'Britain is run by a clique of ex-public school toffs, says a new report.' That was the opening paragraph of *The Sun*'s story about a paper we published in 2005 on the educational backgrounds of the nation's MPs. The headline above it:

TOFFS ARE RUNNING COUNTRY.

Now, I'm not sure the word 'toff' appeared anywhere in our report.†

But there was no distortion of the report's central claim. When we looked into it, we found that almost a third of the MPs sitting in government in 2005 were privately educated. That was compared with about 7 per cent in the population at large. It was even more pronounced in the House of Lords: 62 per cent of them had gone to private

---

* The second time I came across Murdoch was at the River Café in Hammersmith in 2011, on the evening after he had appeared in Parliament before the phone-hacking inquiry. That day his then wife, Wendi Deng, had bravely intervened to protect him from the attentions of a custard pie-throwing protestor. It surprised me to find their party sitting at an open table in the crowded restaurant. I thought they might have preferred somewhere more secluded in the circumstances. Unfortunately for them, the River Café's private room had been booked that night ... by me. I nodded in acknowledgement, shuffled sheepishly past and through the door.

† 'The Educational Backgrounds of Members of the House of Commons and the House of Lords'. The Sutton Trust, December 2005.

schools, and 13 per cent of them to just one of those private schools. Can you guess which one? I'm sure you can. There were almost as many Lords who had been to Eton as there were Lords who had been to comprehensive school – any comprehensive school. It's comprehensive schools, by the way, where 90 per cent of the country get their education. So one school accounted for as many members of upper chamber as over 3,000 state schools.

The products of private schools were not just more likely to make it into the Commons or the Lords; on both sides of the House, they were more likely to hold office. So a double element of advantage appeared to be at work: if you wanted to get into Parliament or to take part in government, it still helped, in the twenty-first century, to be a member of a privileged social caste.

Obviously I would never suggest that political leaders are unelectable simply because their parents sent them to a private school. Winston Churchill, after all, went to Harrow, and he didn't do too badly. But it was about numbers. If the educational and social background of so many of our legislators was so unrepresentative of the country as a whole, what were the chances they would understand the educational struggles and aspirations of the 90 per cent of parents for whom going private wasn't an option? Who were you going to trust to legislate on state education? MPs? How much experience of it did they actually have? The sight of so many MPs and peers voting on a state system in which they (and often their sons and daughters) had no direct personal stake was hardly reassuring. Could it be coincidence that legislators in countries whose educational achievements were so often more impressive than the UK's were more likely to have been to state schools themselves and to send their children there?

With one simple but honed and carefully aimed piece of research, the Sutton Trust was able to open up big questions like these and spark a national conversation.

We had Doug Thomson on board now as Director of Development, a key hire, and Lee Elliot Major, who had previously been with *The Guardian* and *The Times Higher Educational Supplement*. Lee became our Director of Research and ultimately our Chief Executive.

We began a 'Leading People' survey, looking at the educational backgrounds of top people. Those surveys perpetually threw up striking numbers: our most recent one looked at 5,000 top people and found that 40 per cent of them went to private school and 25 per cent to Oxbridge. I find that staggering. As snapshots of social immobility, these surveys were eye-catching and impressive. They routinely hit the front pages: 'Private Schools Retain Their Grip on Britain's Leading Professions', as a headline from 2016 put it.

Going further, we produced a 'Mobility Manifesto' ahead of the 2010 general election, and we repeated it for the elections of 2015 and 2019. The areas where it urged action included fair access to universities, including the introduction of post-qualification applications; the banning of unpaid internships, which are socially iniquitous and encourage closed shops; the creation of broader pathways to the most sought-after jobs; open access to independent day schools; and the development of essential life skills – things like motivation, confidence, communication, self-control and stress-management. Ninety-four per cent of employers were telling us that essential life skills were at least as important, if not more important, as academic qualifications. Yet for the most part private schools seemed to have the scope and resources to devote significant time to better develop those skills in their kids.

As part of a broader picture in which low- and moderate-income kids don't get the opportunity to develop the life skills that can take them forward, this matters massively. Our reporting has amply demonstrated that if you are assertive, talkative, enthusiastic and unintimidated in social settings, you are far more likely to earn more than people who are none of those things. That's probably obvious enough. But also, if you are assertive, talkative, enthusiastic and unintimidated, there is something else that can be assumed about you: that you are likely to be from a well-off background. In the UK, assertion, eloquence and enthusiasm are enjoyed by, and nurtured within, a privileged class. This is how a society ends up setting like concrete.

Along the way, the Sutton Trust turned its attention to the judiciary. Three out of four top judges, over two-thirds of leading barristers and more than half the partners at top law firms turned out to be privately educated.*

* 'The Educational Backgrounds of the UK's Top Solicitors, Barristers and Judges', The Sutton Trust, May 2005.

We got together with Nigel Savage, the chief executive of the College of Law (and someone who himself left school at 16), and talked about how to widen access to the law. The result was Pathways to Law, a programme which aimed to identify potential lawyers while they were still at school and give them practical help on the way to a place at law school that might have been out of reach to them otherwise. The College of Law stumped up £1.25 million over five years and we put in £250,000. The idea was to run an extended summer school-type programme with five universities – Manchester, Leeds, Southampton, Warwick and the LSE – all twinned with a nearby College of Law. Our traditional criteria applied: the students, fifty at each university, were to be chosen from the worst-performing schools and from low-income families with no history of university attendance, and they had to be genuine candidates. They attended a programme of careers days, work placements, law seminars and advice sessions, and the idea was that they would go on to be accepted onto good law courses and to qualify as lawyers. The programme was a huge success and we expanded it into other professions – medicine, banking, finance. Our Pathways programmes, which are still growing, now support 800 sixth-form students each year in attempting to access highly competitive professions that were blocked to them.

After the election of 2017, we were able to report that more than half of MPs had been to comprehensive schools. Only 29 per cent of them had been privately educated, down from 32 per cent in 2015. The Parliamentary Privilege 2017 brief found that 52 per cent of the House had been state educated, compared with 49 per cent in 2015. Things appeared to be going in the right direction. However, MPs were still four times as likely to have been to a fee-paying school than a state school.

Also in 2017, the number of state school pupils admitted to Oxbridge rose to 58 per cent (Oxford) and 62.5 per cent (Cambridge). The figure went up again in 2018/19, when Oxford was 60.5 per cent state and Cambridge was 65 per cent. That was encouraging. In 1997, when I founded the Trust, Oxford was just 47 per cent state and Cambridge was 51 per cent. We had led the way in working with them to diversify their social intakes and in urging them to get out there and cast their nets more widely, and we had clearly made a difference. But there was so much more still to do.

Of course, not everything I attempted at this time went entirely to plan. I was asked to work with Eric Thomas, the vice-chancellor of Bristol University, to look at university fund-raising and explore what UK universities could learn from their US counterparts. We agreed it would be good to take a group of university vice-chancellors out to the States and do a tour of some of their universities, so that we could observe how their fund-raising operations functioned on the ground. I figured that would be better than sitting around a table in England, trying to talk about it in the abstract. Nobody else seemed terribly keen on the idea, though, until I said that I would hire a private jet to get us around while we were out there. For some reason that seemed to increase people's enthusiasm. Suddenly university vice-chancellors were scrambling to sign up.

So a party of six vice-chancellors came out to Palm Beach and joined me at my house for dinner, and the following morning we boarded the very comfortable private jet that I had hired and flew to the first stop on our tour – the University of Florida at Gainsville. This was the first time on a private jet for many, if not all, of the visiting party, and I sensed that they were rather enjoying it.

After some meetings and presentations in Gainsville and a good night's sleep, we went back to the airport in the morning and reboarded, ready to jet off in style to our second stop – Penn State. Unfortunately our deluxe plane chose this moment to have an electrical meltdown. It wouldn't budge. After a long time sitting on the tarmac and getting hot, we all had to stumble off and hang around in the airport while a replacement was sourced. It was the best part of a day before a second, and much less comfortable, plane was found to take us onwards, by which time the mood had turned a little grubby.

Still, we eventually got to Penn State, where we were treated to a college basketball game against Michigan, and where seats in the arena were ruthlessly distributed entirely according to how much a person had donated to the university. Those who had dug deepest were courtside; those who had been less generous to their alma mater were stuck out somewhere behind the backboard. It was that stark.

But in every respect these US institutions were clearly light years ahead of the UK when it came to generating funding and devoted huge energy to it. One important theme was the importance of 'senior-year giving' – encouraging alumni to become benefactors even while they were still in their final year. At Johns Hopkins in Baltimore, the name of Michael Bloomberg inevitably came up in this context. Mike is a generous supporter of the Sutton Trust and I consider him a good friend. My wife Susan and I have enjoyed playing golf with Mike and his partner Diana and have spent time at his estate in Southampton, New York.

On tour with the vice-chancellors we learned that Mike had given Johns Hopkins a small donation when he graduated. By 2018, following the huge success of Bloomberg LP, he was in a position to give the school $1.8 billion, the largest ever single contribution to an American academic institution.* It's clearly worth cultivating your alumni early.

Back at the Trust, our area of influence grew in 2011 after I had some extensive conversations with Michael

---

* That gift is devoted to undergraduate financial aid and the funding of needs-blind admissions. Mike spoke very much after my own heart when he wrote, in an op ed for *The New York Times* that coincided with that donation: 'America is at its best when we reward people based on the quality of their work, not the size of their pocketbook. Denying students entry to a college based on their ability to pay undermines equal opportunity. And it strikes at the heart of the American dream: the idea that every person, from every community, has the chance to rise based on merit.'

Gove. The government was looking for ways to increase the attainment levels of the poorest pupils in the most challenging schools, and it was putting out a tender for a non-profit organization to get schools doing innovative things in that area that could spread through the system. The idea was essentially to create an educational R&D department. The budget was £125 million with a 15-year spend-down. We were asked to bid. It sounded as though it would be the perfect complement to the Trust's work with poorer children at the top end of the system, so we put our hat in the ring. So did 14 other interested parties.

We got through the first round of bidding. That left five organizations in the field. At the key meetings I made the point that I had invested tens of millions of my own money in the Sutton Trust, which indicated how serious I was. We ended up winning the bid.

So that led to the Sutton Trust, as lead partner, establishing the Education Endowment Foundation, with help from Impetus, a private equity charity. I've been chairman of the EEF since its inception. The staff of the EEF crammed in with us on the ninth floor at Millbank for a while, then moved down to some space of their own on the fifth. James Turner was interim CEO for seven months until Kevan Collins joined. James had joined the Trust as one of Tessa Stone's formative recruitments after spells with the Charity Commission and the Labour Party, and he was another of the outstanding (and shockingly young) hires that were responsible for pushing the Trust onward. He came back eventually to be CEO of the Trust. Under Kevan's guidance, the EEF began raising the bar for educational research in England, funding programmes and evaluations. In January 2020, the Foundation was able to celebrate the publication of its 100th result from randomized control trials in UK schools, meaning that it was conducting more controlled trials in education than any other organization globally.

To be granted management of the EEF and its £125 million budget was solid proof of the Trust's standing. At the same time, it was the opposite of the way we wanted to go as the Sutton Trust. We've had offers of government money at various times to develop various Sutton Trust programmes, but I've always said 'no' to it, and I always will, because then we can guarantee our independence and be as critical of government as a foundation like ours needs to be.

From that position of independence, the Trust can continue with its mission to nudge British education towards greater and greater fairness, calling out the disparities in the system and digging, in particular, into the corners in which privilege operates more obscurely. For example, in 2019 we published a report that shone a light on the number of parents paying for extra tuition for their kids, and the way in which that was again widening the gap between the education of rich and poor.* Twenty-seven per cent of secondary pupils were receiving extra lessons from private tutors at home, up from 20 per cent in 2010. At tuition rates of £28 per hour these were mainly pupils with well off

---

* 'Private Tuition 2019', The Sutton Trust, September 2019.

parents. State school children in London were almost twice as likely to be tutored as kids elsewhere. And one in four state school teachers had tutored privately outside school. Again, it was a way in which wealth operated covertly to reinforce privilege, and it needed to be highlighted and monitored and, if at all possible, compensated for elsewhere in the system.

Then there was the pernicious problem of covert selection in state schools. In 2006, I paid a visit to two schools in west London: the London Oratory and the Phoenix High School. They were both comprehensives, yet they had very different social mixes. Of the 1,338 pupils at the Oratory at that time, only 7.9 per cent were eligible for free school meals, way below the national average of 14.3 per cent. At the Phoenix, it was a stunning 56 per cent.

What marks those schools out is that the London Oratory is a faith school. It's the Roman Catholic institution to which Tony Blair, the former Labour Prime Minister, sent his three eldest children. It's a very fine school, but historically if you wanted to have a realistic chance of getting in there, you would most likely have needed to have shown that you were a regular churchgoer and played an active part in your parish.

It's selection by stealth, and this tends to be what happens when schools are in charge of their own admissions. Academy schools are rife with it, too. We looked into it. Schools left to run the selection of their own pupils averaged 7.9 per cent of pupils eligible for free school meals compared with 13.7 per cent in their local areas. The biggest gap of all was in faith schools: 5.6 per cent on average compared with 14.6 per cent for their local areas.

At the time of writing, in early 2020, the Trust gives 5,000 high-potential low- and moderate-income young people each year the opportunity to change their lives. To date, 50,000 children have had their futures directly impacted on by what we do. Some charities specialize in research. Some charities specialize in programmatic intervention. And some charities specialize in policy influence. The Sutton Trust, uniquely, covers all three, and we have gained enormous credibility in each of these areas. By our estimates we have influenced government policy on an amazing 34 occasions. We have published over 200 research reports on education and social mobility issues, and I don't think it's an exaggeration to say that the Sutton Trust has put social mobility on the map. It was a term that had little currency when we began. Indeed, before we started bashing on about it, if you had asked people what they thought social mobility was, a lot of them would probably have guessed it had something to do with bus services for the elderly. In 2003, Hansard could record just nine references to it across the House of Commons and the House of Lords in that parliamentary year, and no debates on the topic. In 2018, 13 years after our first big report, there were 424 references to it, and 15 different debates. Our pressure, amongst others, triggered the creation of annual social mobility indicators in 2011 and led to the establishment of the Social Mobility Commission, an independent body that monitors social mobility across the UK and promotes its improvement.

In 2003, I was knighted. Let me dispel a myth about that ceremony: when you are kneeling in front of the Queen and she's finished tapping you on the shoulders with the sword, she does not say, 'Arise, Sir Peter.' That was a bit of a disappointment.

I suppose I'm sceptical about the honours system generally. But the knighthood tends to go over well at the golf club I belong to. There are a lot of successful people there, but very few knights. Automatic flight upgrades for people with titles, though? That's another myth. Reservations at restaurants and a decent table are about all you get.

On top of the knighthood, and the building named after me at Oxford, I have also been the recipient of 20 honorary degrees: honorary doctorates, honorary fellowships. I like to make the point in my acceptance speech that people talk about grade inflation in GCSEs, grade inflation in A levels and inflation in degree classes, but there is one place where there has been no grade inflation at all: honorary degrees.

In some ways, I made a break with my entrepreneurial past. In other ways, I didn't at all. The way we manage the Trust is entirely consistent with the way I managed when I was a business consultant. The Trust gets run the exact same way I would run a company: we focus on the data, we're strategic and we pour our effort into the things that will genuinely make a difference. And we look for high returns. If you're working with 17-year-olds and changing the directions their lives take – well, to my way of thinking, that's a high leverage point. We bring a business rigour to it: high leverage, high impact, a focus on efficiency, measuring the effectiveness of everything we do, making sure the money that comes in the door goes out again to the maximum effect. After all, for about 15 years it was my own money, so I made damn sure it was well spent. In 2019, the Trust invested £4 million in programmes and generated an estimated £56 million of value for our students. That figure increases every year as we invest more money. We are very fortunate to have Ian Walsh, a Managing Director and Senior Partner at the Boston Consulting Group, as a member of our board, and hugely indebted to BCG for the analysis they do for us *pro bono* as part of their corporate responsibility initiative.* BCG have worked out that every £1 invested by the Trust results in £14 of value for our beneficiaries. That's incredible leverage.

I'm proud of those numbers, and I'm also proud that this is how we think about what we do – that this is how we measure it. Other charities don't do that sum, and, even if they did, I doubt the numbers would be as impressive. The focus on impact and value for money is more mainstream in the charity sector now than it was, but it's still by no means the rule. The Trust has never done it any other way.

---

* When I was at BCG, nobody was interested in doing non-profit work. Bruce Henderson actually took us out of it. Now people clamour to work *pro bono*. I'm extremely glad they do.

People are often surprised when they visit the office at Millbank. They expect there to be a hundred or so people beavering away in there. Actually, it's 30 these days, but I understand why people misread it. We have something that's enormously valuable to a medium-size philanthropic organization: a footprint way beyond our shoe size. If we do something, it gets a lot of coverage. When an education story comes up, the media want to know what I and the Trust think about it, whether it's school buses (they make a lot of sense, I reckon), or someone who wants to found a scholarship exclusively for white kids (tricky). We average more than 800 mentions in the national media every year, more than two a day on average, and thousands in the local press. Our brand is as strong as, or stronger than, that of far bigger charities. On education and social mobility, we have become the prime source for an informed and entirely independent position.

I've been at the helm of this for more than 20 years now, and I've put in approximately £50 million of my own money. In addition, we have raised a further £60 million – a big number. Our next step is to raise a significant endowment, something which will ensure that the Trust carries on doing what it does after I'm gone. Not that I have any plans to go anywhere (my father, by the way, is 100 and my mother 95).

Meanwhile the entrance to the Department for Education must have one of the fastest revolving doors in government. In the 23 years of the Sutton Trust, no fewer than 12 ministers have held the job of Secretary of State for

Education (as the role is now referred to, though even the job title seems to change with unnerving frequency: Secretary of State for Education and Science, Secretary of State for Education and Employment, Secretary of State for Education and Skills, Secretary of State for Children, Schools and Families – you name it, the Minister for Education has been called it). Most of those ministers have survived for less than two years. The only two long-serving ministers have been David Blunkett and Michael Gove, who served a combined total of nine years. So if you take them out, the rest served an average of 21 months.

Still, if that allows me to become a still point at the centre of this world, a comparatively constant presence, then great. In 2012, at a lunch to celebrate 15 years of the Trust, I sat between David Blunkett and Michael Gove. Each of those two was a figure of unusual persistence as far as the Trust was concerned – a permanent feature of the landscape, almost. But I was even more persistent, as far as they were concerned. During lunch, Blunkett turned to me and said, in his thick Sheffield accent, 'The thing that impresses me about you, Peter, is that you've *stook at it*.'

Put that on my tombstone: 'He stook at it.'

15

MY VANISHING ACT. AND MY REAPPEARING ACT

It was the front-page story in the London *Evening Standard*. The posters on the stands read:

NEWS EXTRA: LONDON CHARITY TYCOON VANISHES.

I wonder if I saw those posters. It's perfectly possible. I must have passed places where they were on display that Monday afternoon. But I wouldn't know. I remember almost nothing about the 48 hours for which I disappeared.

So, we reach the low point of this story – the literal low point: my brush with depression. Luckily for me, this is no longer a taboo topic. For the greater part of my life, what happened to me in 2009 would have been nothing I could talk about. But that's changing, and I'm glad it's changing, and if I can help in any way to continue to soften that taboo, I will. Because not talking about depression is just about the best way to go about encouraging depression.

From the outside, it could have seemed to come from nowhere. People might easily have said, 'What's *he* got to be depressed about? He's Britain's leading educational philanthropist ... although, now you mention it, we can't think of another one.'

And before I was depressed, I would have been making the same sort of assumption. Like everybody else who has a run-in with this illness, I never thought I would be the kind of person who would become seriously depressed. But I was wrong.

Karen had come into my office one day and said she wanted to get a divorce. It wasn't a surprise – the relationship had gone wrong, we were getting on badly. But the children were young and I thought we should try and stay together somehow for them. Karen disagreed. I went to a solicitor to find out what my options were and the solicitor told me: 'Stay in the house. If you leave the house, the chances are you will lose it, and if you lose the house, it's almost certainly going to complicate your access to the children.'

This was probably good legal advice. But as psychiatric advice, it turned out to be terrible.

I stayed put, and it was a disaster. Living in a house with someone who is increasingly keen that you shouldn't live in that house is no recipe for contentment. The atmosphere was constantly virulent. It went on for six very long months and I got lower and lower until I became depressed. Eventually I became so depressed that I did leave the house – but only in order to check into the Priory Hospital in Roehampton.

This was a good move to the extent that it brought me into the orbit of Dr Barbara Rooney, a psychiatrist who would end up helping me boundlessly. In other ways, though, the Priory was a bad move. OK, the place obviously works for some people. But not, broadly speaking, for me. I don't know what I did all day. You've got a room, you sit around in it. There's a lawn outside, but everyone goes there to smoke, so it's as much cigarette butts as grass. You get medicine. You're supposed to go to therapy, but I was instinctively sceptical. I'm a physical scientist, so I struggle to believe in that stuff. There was a lot of sitting about on the floor and stretching. There were a few familiar faces around: a rock star, a retired footballer. I suppose, in other circumstances, that might have lent it something. But I thought it was a bloody awful place. I don't know why I ended up there, really … except that this seemed to be what you did if you were depressed and you'd got some money. 'Put him in the Priory!'

I was there for several weeks. When I came out, I wasn't much better, and now Karen had taken over the house. I couldn't get back in. The fact that I had depression was, she felt, a reason to exclude me almost completely. I was locked out. I could only see the children for three hours on a Sunday evening. None of this exactly raised my spirits. In fact, by this point I was floundering.

Anna, my assistant, God bless her, rented a house for me in Arthur Road in Wimbledon and fixed it up with some basic furniture. And my parents came and stayed with me for a while. They were heroic. They took care of me. Work was on hold. I had stopped going into the office. Instead, I would sit in the house, in a mental fog, and stare. The big item on the agenda for the day was walking around the block. My parents would encourage me. Sometimes I'd start out and then, after a couple of hundred yards, give up and return home. Sometimes I wouldn't make it out of the door at all. Depression gets this awful grip on you and it won't let go. The outlook is bleak, everything is black. You're pessimistic about everything, you don't want to do anything – it's just a horrible state to be in.

I hit bottom on a Sunday morning in February 2009. Karen had taken the children to Florida for the half-term holiday. Without saying anything to anyone about where I was going, I got up and walked out the front door.

I don't know why I did it, or what purpose I had in mind, or if I even had a purpose. Something in me simply said, 'You've got to get out of here.' So, at about 8.30 a.m., I left the house and went down the hill to Wimbledon Park. I think I may have sat on a bench in the park for a while. I also have a vague recollection of eventually walking to the nearby tube station and getting on a train. I didn't take a jacket or a coat – I was wearing a shirt and jumper – and this in the middle of February. After that, I remember nothing, literally nothing, until I vaguely recall a conversation with somebody at Victoria train station.

It was soon after 11 a.m., on Tuesday morning and I had been missing for 48 hours.

By that point, the story was in the national papers. In *The Mirror*: 'Family fears for missing philanthropist Sir Peter Lampl, 61.' In *The Times*: 'Appeal by police as depressed Sir Peter Lampl goes missing.' In the *Daily Express*: 'Fears grow over missing philanthropist.'

Merton police put out a statement on the Monday morning, saying that I had walked out the previous day and that my family was 'very concerned' for my safety. Reporters were soon outside the house in Wimbledon, and at this point at least the story managed to take a darkly funny turn. My father wasn't especially media savvy – and why would he be? Without fully appreciating, perhaps, how British tabloid news-gathering works, he seems to have got into a fairly garrulous conversation on a park bench with a journalist from the *Daily Mail* in which he related how he had played golf with me recently and that I'd been upset about how badly I was playing (not that unusual, actually). According to my dad, I'd been wondering whether the medication I'd been taking had anything to do with it. And apparently I'd said something about how I was going to go to the doctor and get it sorted out.

This stuff must have been manna to a jobbing reporter on a tight deadline. The line that appeared in the *Daily Mail* was: 'The millionaire philanthropist vanished after switching his medication for depression in an attempt to improve his golf swing.'

Quite a tale: entrepreneur disappears off the radar

because he's upset about how his tablets are causing him to hook it left. So let me state once and for all, for the record: golf played no part in this personal drama.

Two days passed – days in which I guess I must have wandered around London, and perhaps sat around, though I don't recall any of that wandering or any of that sitting. Eventually, on the Tuesday morning, someone recognized me at Victoria station. I have only the vaguest recollection of this moment; I was still lost in a fog. But a woman noticed me sitting on a bench, apparently looking very distressed, and came and spoke to me.

Some of the newspaper reports set this scene in a station café and had the woman reading in her newspaper about the missing millionaire philanthropist and then lowering her paper to find herself looking across the room at – could it possibly be? Yes! – the missing millionaire philanthropist himself. Which would have been perfect if it had been a movie.

In fact, the bench I was sitting on was on the station concourse, and the woman knew me. She was Christine Ryan and at the time she was the chief inspector and CEO of the Independent Schools Inspectorate, so our paths had crossed a number of times, albeit in more formal settings and when I wasn't on the police's missing persons list. She must have been passing through Victoria on her way to a meeting or something, and there I was, in a mess.

Christine left me in the care of some British Transport Police officers. It seems I was taken upstairs to some kind of room in the station and phone calls were made – to my sister, Erica, and to Anna in the office. Anna had to come down to the station with my passport, to prove my identity, and some money, because I didn't have any on me. Then she took me in a taxi to Erica's flat in Parsons Green.

The headline in the next day's *Times*: 'Missing philanthropist Sir Peter Lampl found alive.'

A couple of weeks later, an enormous bill arrived from Dial-a-Cab, the car service. So that solved the mystery of my whereabouts on my two lost nights: I appeared to have spent them circling London in taxis on my account.

I had caused a lot of people a lot of worry. 'Fears grow for missing philanthropist.' Fears had grown. I had gone missing while depressed, and all the people close to me had had to consider the possibility that I might have gone away to end it all. Reflecting on what I had put others through – my parents, Erica, the children – was a big part of escaping the fog I began to crawl out from under. Increasingly, there were signs of recovery. One of these came when I was persuaded to go with my niece, Rosie, to see a production of *West Side Story* at Wimbledon Theatre. For one thing, when the depression had a grip, I wouldn't have done that. Secondly, I not only went, but I clearly enjoyed it. Who doesn't like *West Side Story*?

In time, I was on an even keel again, and back at work. But there was still a divorce to get through and custody to arrange. The deal for men in the UK seems outrageous to me. You are thought to have cut a good deal if you get access to your children every other weekend and half of the school holidays. But that means you never see them on a school day. You never see them in the morning before school or when they came home after school – like those might not be really important times for a parent to be with his children. It's a Stone Age arrangement. If you get divorced in Florida, it's usually a 50–50 split – both of money and time with the children. Here, nothing even close to that. And the assumption underpinning it is that men have no significant part to play in the rearing of their children. It's wrong.

But it's the law. And I had to take Karen to court to secure access to the kids. That was horrific. The kids had to be interviewed by a court-appointed officer to find out how they felt about things. Katie was 13, Chris was 11 and Steph was eight: it was a horrible thing to put them through. Yet without question the happiest day of my life was after that, when the court-appointed officer came into the court room and told the judge, 'All three said they wanted to see more of their dad.' I broke down and cried.

So I was making some headway. I was getting court-stipulated regular access to the kids every other weekend and some holidays. I took Steph and Chris to Venice, showed them the city where the streets are full of water. Things were opening up. But then another terrible twist: Karen's brother-in-law Greg called to tell me that she was ill – seriously ill. It was pancreatic cancer. Obviously our legal battle stopped there, while she was treated. She insisted it wouldn't get the better of her. Or maybe she was in denial. But pancreatic cancer is lethal, merciless. Fourteen months later, my children lost their mother.

So that was a period of immense darkness. And I saw none of it coming. But once again, we return to this point: there are always discontinuities. You'll assume that you're going to run along the same path. But there is usually something coming out of left field to spin you off in another direction. Nothing you can do but try and deal with it when it happens.

I got better. I was fortunate to have people who could help me with that: Dr Rooney, Anna, Erica, my parents, my children. And Susan Hollo. Susan was executive director of the Els for Autism Foundation, the charity founded by the world-famous golfer Ernie Els. Our paths had crossed a little in Florida, where our kids had briefly gone to the same school. Somewhere around 2005, we had once sat next to each other at a dinner party, where I think I talked too much about Open Access. Five years later, in 2010, we were both separated. A friend told me I should call her. So I did and we went out for dinner a couple of times.

We began to see each other regularly after that, or as regularly as we could, given that we were on different continents a lot of the time. We probably saw each other once every six weeks for a year and a half. Eventually, one evening in the Rhythm Café, a restaurant in Palm Beach, I said: 'You know I want to marry you, don't you?'

We had both done big weddings. We were now fans of big elopements. We flew to Stellenbosch in South Africa, where a minister married us on the patio of Ernie Els' wonderful winery. Then we flew back to London and set up home in Chelsea.

We needed an American base so we took a lease on a place in Palm Beach. Over the wall at the bottom of our garden is Mar-a-Lago, Trump's so-called Winter White House. But otherwise it's a very nice neighbourhood.

The day Karen died, my kids moved in with us, along with two cats and a dog. It will tell you a lot about the kind of person Susan is that she didn't even flinch. On the contrary, she opened her arms. She already had three kids, one close in age to mine and two older ones, so we became a large blended family.

Susan plays golf better than I ever will. In fact she does an awful lot of things better than I ever will. We've been married for eight years and I'm thrilled to have found such a wonderful person to share my life with. Very few people are as lucky.

16

ENTREPRENEURIAL PHILANTHROPY FOR ALL

Aristotle once said: 'To give away money is an easy matter and in any man's power. But to decide to whom to give it, and how much, and when, and for what purpose and how, is neither in every man's power nor an easy matter.'

I would only add, 'Don't let that stop you, though.'

Whether it's the ancient philosophical complications that put them off, or whether it's other reasons, it's clearly the case that high net-worth individuals in the UK don't find giving away money to be 'an easy matter'. They certainly don't find it as easy as they should do. Britain is a long way behind America in this area. When it comes to philanthropic giving, the UK could, and should, be doing a lot better.

At the end of 2019, the Sutton Trust, in association with Public First, did some research into public perceptions about philanthropy in Britain, and perhaps the most striking outcome was that four out of ten British people didn't know the meaning of the word. Literally. Press them on what philanthropy means, and a disappointingly large portion of Brits will most likely hazard a guess that it's got something to do with stamp-collecting.

Of course, there's a simpler word: 'charity'. Probably everybody knows what charity is. But, for all their similarities, charity and philanthropy are not the same thing. In fact, they represent radically different approaches to giving money away.

Among the wealthy, charity might be, for instance, something that happens at black-tie fund-raising evenings. I've been to a few of those, in particular while I was living in New York. You will normally be invited along to some giant chandelier-hung hotel ballroom, or possibly a cavernous conference centre somewhere on the West Side. And there will probably be an envelope on the table for you to stuff with money. You will be served three courses, at least one of which will feature chicken. The after-dinner entertainment will be provided by someone like Rod Stewart. And there will generally be a charity auction where the lots are things like the use of someone's private jet, or two weeks on somebody else's private island, or lunch with Henry Kissinger. You'll be treated to the sight of Wall Street hedge-fund managers ostentatiously bidding against each other for gold-leaf spa treatments in Bali, or whatever. Which is kind of gross. And there will be lots of glossy people there who want to be seen, and especially to be seen being charitable.

It's a game. And that's fine, of course. There are worse games rich people could be playing. By the end of the night, no doubt thousands of dollars will have been raised for some good cause or other, and, to some extent, that's where all objections have to end. In the face of a big stack of cash going somewhere it's needed, why get bogged down in arguing about the purity of people's motives?

Although, by the way, those events aren't great ways to raise money. There's so much effort and expense involved in staging them that they don't often end up being cost-efficient. No major university would hold them. Knowing a thing or two about raising and tending endowments, universities realize that splashy one-off nights with a compère off the television and a song from Lionel Richie aren't ultimately where the big donated money lies. That's why they devote themselves to the slower and more patient business of relationship-building.

But anyway, all that aside, my point is that there's an important distinction between charity and philanthropy – and, by extension, a big difference between thinking charitably and thinking philanthropically. We could express it like this: Charity writes a cheque and walks away – job done. Philanthropy writes a cheque and then applies itself to managing the way the cheque gets spent – job just beginning. And it's philanthropy that I think we should be doing much more of in Britain.

Why are Americans so much better at giving money away – both charitably and philanthropically – than Brits? Why do high net-worth individuals there donate so much more, and so much more readily, than their British counterparts? No doubt there are all sorts of cultural reasons.

For instance, in the UK there's a lot of squirrelling money away for the kids to inherit (or for the grandchildren, thus skipping the inheritance tax) – a kind of 'old money' view of the accumulation of wealth. There's no question, too, that national characteristics come into it. In some ways, 'don't flaunt it' is an unhelpful strain in the British character. In my constant quest for funding for the Sutton Trust, I ask British people for money all the time. Many are extremely generous, of course – and obviously I'm grateful to each and every one I come across. I'm particularly grateful to our 110 donors to the Sutton Trust. But sometimes I ask British people for money and it's the last conversation I have with them.

Americans are less troubled about asking for money than Brits tend to be. I learned this truth very graphically when my kids were small and at a tiny school in Florida. One term we got a letter about the school's annual fund-raising drive. Contributions were being solicited, and it was a wealthy community, so the school would have been mad not to ask. I thought about it quite hard, because I wanted to get it right and I didn't want to disappoint anyone, and, after much reflection, I wrote a cheque for $1,000, which I felt was on the generous side, but without being embarrassingly showy. I sent it over. Duty done.

Two days later, my phone rang. It was the school's development director. The first thing to note, of course, is that the school had such a thing. I'm fairly sure I've never come across a kindergarten in the UK that has its own development director. By contrast, Oxford University had just sent me a form letter – a different approach. Anyway, I assumed this guy was calling to thank me for giving so generously and I waited for him to start singing his hymn of gratitude.

On the contrary.

'The Evans family, three houses down from you, have given $5,000,' said the development director, who was an alumnus, by the way. 'So have the Kellys, across the way. I'm sure you don't want to be out of line ...'

My instinctive reaction to this was outrage. I'd sent him $1,000, for God's sake! And he was coming after me for *more*?

At the same time, though, I had to concede the guy had a point. A thousand bucks *wasn't* that much in the broader scheme of things. I listened to his pitch a little longer. Eventually I was talked into funding a scholarship and ended up giving well over $100,000.

Asking for money in the US clearly works.

It doesn't really surprise me, then, that the level of giving as a percentage of gross domestic product is three times as much in the US as it is in the UK. The staggering fact is, if we Brits gave at American levels, we would generate an additional £45 billion each year to spend on good causes. Brits have a lot to learn. We need to get better at asking for donations. And we need to get better at being asked.

Beyond that, we need to get better at philanthropy, in the sense of proper, plugged-in, engaged philanthropy – entrepreneurial philanthropy. By which I mean the kind of organized endeavour that doesn't simply attempt to alleviate the symptoms of a problem by charitably lobbing some money at it, but does something more long term and closely managed to tackle the causes of the problem. This is something that successful entrepreneurs are well placed to do. You could even say it's something they should feel obliged to do.

It seems to have been understood, in the late nineteenth and early twentieth century in America, in the time of Andrew Carnegie and John D. Rockefeller, that if you were a pioneer in business then you would automatically be a pioneer in philanthropy. Carnegie (who was Scottish by birth) wrote about philanthropy as a duty: the wealthy entrepreneur, in his opinion, was merely a 'trustee' of the fortune he had accumulated, and the rich were honour bound to perform the task of 'returning surplus wealth to the mass of their fellows'.* At the same time, Carnegie cautioned against 'indiscriminate charity', describing it as 'one of the serious obstacles to the improvement of our race'. The man who single-mindedly built the vastest steel empire the world had ever known spent the last 20 years of his life employing the same driven talents in the construction of a massive network of philanthropic enterprises.

Similarly, Rockefeller, who is widely considered to be the wealthiest American of all time, used the 40 years for which

* 'The Gospel of Wealth', 1889. In that essay, Carnegie is also scathing about handing fortunes down to the kids. 'It is not well for the children that they should be so burdened,' he writes, urging the wealthy to regard family bequests as 'an improper use of their means'. It is estimated that by the time he died, Carnegie had given away 90 per cent of his fortune, a sum of at least $65 billion in 2019 terms.

he was technically in retirement to turn the shrewd mind of an oil magnate to the business of carefully targeted philanthropy. As the entrepreneur and author Jacqueline Novogratz has written, 'Rockefeller viewed his philanthropy through the lens of his business ... It was highly centralised, it was top down, it was based on experts, and it was big-picture.' For the likes of Rockefeller and Carnegie, philanthropy wasn't a soft sideline to their business: philanthropy *was* their business.

Somewhere in the intervening years, however, that fundamental connection between business and philanthropy got lost – to the point, indeed, where Professor Michael E. Porter of the Harvard Business School was very recently in a position to point out: 'Billions are wasted on ineffective philanthropy. Philanthropy is decades behind business in applying rigorous thinking to the use of money.'

There are shining exceptions, of course. This is true of Mike Bloomberg with Bloomberg Philanthropies. The same is true of Bill Gates, with the Bill & Melinda Gates Foundation. Yet we still see far too many examples of 'ineffective philanthropy' – hands-off, under-managed philanthropy, the kind of philanthropy where the donor's involvement begins and ends with the giving of a sum of money. That mindset needs to change, and I think we've been changing it with our work at the Sutton Trust.

So many charitable concerns nowadays don't properly quantify what they do. They're spending money in a charitable cause and that seems to be regarded as enough in itself. Because it's philanthropy, and philanthropy is inherently a good thing, the rules that would inform the spending of money in other areas of business aren't felt to apply in quite the same way. But, like any other company, a philanthropic organization needs to be accountable. We've been very hot on this right from the beginning. I didn't just pump money into the Sutton Trust from a distance; I made it my business to understand what was going on, to stay on top of it, to manage the spending strategy in association with a set of formidable and equally engaged board members, trustees and donors who shared the Trust's vision, and to make sure that the money I was putting in was working as hard as it possibly could. Whatever your net worth, you only have a finite amount of money, after all. You want to make the most of it. And to do that, I stayed in charge and applied the strategies I had learned as an entrepreneur. I ran the Sutton Trust the way I ran the Sutton Company. Consequently, just as there was leverage in the deals I did with the Sutton Company, there is leverage in the Sutton Trust. The £4 million that the Trust spent on programmes in 2018 created an estimated £56 million of value for the students involved.

I think it helps to acknowledge that philanthropy is competitive. Maybe it would be nice to think that it wasn't – that it existed in a cloud of goodness where virtuous causes simply rose to the surface naturally and in an orderly manner. But you have to be realistic about the world in which you are operating. If you're in philanthropy, you're in competition. There is competition for money and for influence with decision-makers. You have to be prepared to bring your best game. You have to be ready to trust expertise over sentiment. You have to apply exactly the same principles that you would apply in business: hire the best people, assemble the best board, focus on the data, know the returns on every programme, get yourself to the fore-front and then never slacken off.

Very often charity suffers from a kind of benign inertia. It's easy, in the non-profit sector, for the foot to come off the gas and for people to relax a bit because, after all, 'We're being good, aren't we?' We're doing 'good things', so why be brassy or sharp-elbowed about it? Constant pushiness could almost be thought of as inappropriate in this sphere. Yet that loss of internal pressure can be cata-strophic for philanthropic organizations. Inertia, benign or otherwise, is the enemy of good business. Suddenly you've got slack in the system and money and time are being wasted. You wouldn't tolerate that slack if you were running a company; you would move in to tighten it at source. So why be any different in a philanthropic organi-zation, where arguably every pound is more precious?

In the UK, we need more entrepreneurs to come into philanthropy and bring their business heads with them. I think there are four simple ways in which they could be encouraged to do so.

First, there's a straightforward legislative step in which the government simplifies the tax treatment of donations. Gift Aid is complex for higher-rate taxpayers, most people don't fully understand it, and the benefit gets shared between the charity and the individual donor. It would be better, in my opinion, to gravitate towards the American way, where philanthropic giving is treated as a straight deduction from income. It's a completely clear system and the donor gets all the tax benefit. It actively incentivizes donations, which is the point.

Secondly, the government should promote far more matched funding schemes. The Education Endowment Foundation is a good example of this – an organization seeded by £125 million of government money, some of which was then matched through fund-raising. Such schemes represent good value for the taxpayer and are attractive to co-funders who are looking for maximum leverage on their donations. Matched funding is also a good way for the government to point philanthropic giving in the direction of the most important issues.

Thirdly, we should instil a greater recognition and celebration of philanthropy. It's peer pressure, clearly, and social expectation that cause high net-worth Americans to give more philanthropically than their British counterparts, and at a younger age. By contrast, very little prominence is given to philanthropy in the UK and generosity frequently goes unremarked and uncelebrated here. You will know the British joke: 'He does a lot for charity, but he doesn't like to talk about it.' Well, maybe it would be a good idea if he *did* like to talk about it at least a little bit more than we do. If we can overcome some of that British bashfulness and squeamishness about giving, we can change the prevailing culture around philanthropy and encourage it to flourish.

Fourthly, and perhaps most importantly, we should work to broaden the definition of philanthropy – and not just so that people can no longer confuse it with stamp collecting. We need to be clear about the ways in which philanthropy is distinct from charity and be clear that it is entrepreneurial by default.

We need to understand, too, that philanthropy can be the giving of *anything* – experience, skills, time … things that any of us may have accrued in the course of our lives. In that sense, entrepreneurial philanthropy ceases to be the preserve of the rich. On the contrary, it can become the business of practically every one of us. What are you rich in? What do you have a lot of? What can you afford to give away, or give back? And, most importantly, what's the best use that you can make of what you have to give? How can you maximally leverage that particular skill of yours, that experience that you have gained in your work or your life, that time you have free on a weekend or in the evening?

There's no cause too small, either. Every time I help some kids with their education, I can guarantee that somebody somewhere will say to me: 'Why aren't you helping *all* the kids?' Well, great idea. Tough one to pull off, though. Yet, just because you can't change everything, it doesn't mean you shouldn't try and change *something* – the one small thing, maybe, that it lies in your power to change. Life is unfair, and life is always going to be unfair. All we can do – indeed, the best we can do – is try and make it a little fairer.

AFTERWORD

On 2020 and beyond

On 2 January 2020, Boris Johnson, who had been elected as prime minister with an 80-seat majority less than a month earlier, used his official Twitter account to post a message saying, 'This is going to be a fantastic year for Britain.'

It didn't quite work out that way.

Twenty-nine days later, the World Health Organization declared a global health emergency, as cases of a contagious respiratory and vascular disease which would shortly be given the name Covid-19 began to surge in almost every corner of the globe. By 23 March, British schools had been ordered to shut indefinitely, pubs, restaurants and gyms were closed, and Johnson was on television instructing Britons to leave their homes only to exercise once a day and buy necessary food and medicine. In April, the UK death rate from Covid-19 rose above 1,000 people per day. The country would remain in lockdown until July 4th and would then impose a variety of local restrictions before locking down again in late autumn in the face of the pandemic's second wave. By that point, more than 60,000 people in the UK had died – the worst excess death rate in Europe – and the country had suffered the largest contraction of its economy (down 20.4 per cent between April and June) since quarterly records began.

So, 2020: how fantastic was it for *you*?

I spent the first lockdown at home in Surrey, along with my daughters, Katie and Steph. I cannot pretend to have suffered. Yes, I missed going into the office; that disruption to a life-long rhythm. But I got to know my daughters better than I could ever have imagined. As well as being excellent company, they turned out to be equally excellent cooks. I ate like a king. I watched all the Bond movies (Roger Moore is my favourite Bond). And I didn't get Covid-19. But of course, isolation comes easily if you own a detached house in the countryside. When your major complaint is that the golf club is closed, it's probably best not to make out that you have endured hardship or lay claim to having summoned the 'Blitz spirit'.

This was, however, a strenuously active time for the Sutton Trust, to put it mildly. To the extent that the pandemic was having a direct impact on education and was clearly going to have extensive, longer-term implications for social mobility, Covid-19 had parked its tanks directly on our lawn. Accordingly, we turned all our efforts to fighting back. We dropped what we were doing and signed up for the national effort. We switched to online working as quickly as possible, shelved our existing research projects and threw our every resource into researching the impact of the pandemic on our areas of concern.

And what that research kept showing was the dire extent to which the pandemic was exacerbating social divisions. The sad truth is that the lockdown between March and July 2020, and the months of missed learning it caused, only served to widen the gap in this country between the poorest and wealthiest students. 'Home schooling' was a fine notion in principle, but, of course, it would depend on the home. Too often those from low-income families found themselves locked down with limited access to computers and the internet, with an absence of quiet places to study and with parents who lacked confidence or time for home schooling – and that was before one factored in the striking differences in the provision of remote teaching offered by the independent and state sectors. It was clear that, not only would those circumstances diminish the immediate opportunities of the affected children, they would set back the whole country. An entire generation of potential talent seemed destined to be skipped over. But there is another aspect to all of this. Education is not a benign activity; it's the principal way nations compete with each other. That we've had a 'bad' epidemic means we've fallen even further behind other countries, exacerbating an already bad situation. This is a serious issue in a number of ways but particularly when you consider our poor standing in the education world.

At the Sutton Trust, our approach, in the midst of all this, was, as ever, both pragmatic and entrepreneurial. We looked on in horror, for example, at the catastrophic mess the government managed to make around the cancellation of public A level exams. But we also seized our chance to press home one of our long-standing and most cherished campaigning goals.

In August, when the government issued its computer-adjusted stand-in exam grades, Ofqual's rightly scorned algorithm was shown to have undervalued the work of bright students in under-performing schools – precisely those students the Sutton Trust had been working since inception to encourage. After a weekend of uproar and bitter protest, the government hastily U-turned, ditched those algorithm-based results and reinstated the predicted grades supplied by teachers at the schools.

But this left university applications in chaos and universities with a giant administrative mess to sweep up. That, too, was deeply regrettable, but it granted us the opportunity to promote resoundingly a shift to post-qualification applications, for which we had been agitating for some time and the wisdom of which now stood emphatically revealed. A world in which students only apply to university when they have their confirmed A level grades in their hands could only look sensible and blessedly straightforward against the backdrop of 2020's mayhem.

Here, still more pertinently, was an opportunity to press home with renewed vigour and clarity the case for Open

Access, our plans for which I discussed in Chapter 13. Years of painfully slow but vitally important progress in closing the attainment gap between the poorest students and their most affluent peers were being reversed before our eyes. As with the A level debacle, one could shake one's head in despair or one could decide that it was time to promote bold, practical interventions. There would perhaps never be a better moment to open up independent schools to anyone with the potential to attend. Over the summer I was able to sit down with Graham Brady, a Conservative MP and chairman of the 1922 Committee, and a long-time supporter of Open Access. Together we were able to come up with a paper which Graham put directly under the prime minister's nose. The time for Open Access could not be riper, and the impact on education and on social mobility would be game-changing for a post-pandemic UK.

During lockdown, like so many of us, I found myself with more time to reflect than I was used to having. And one of the things I found myself reflecting on in particular was that Yorkshire childhood of mine. We were only a few years beyond the horrors of the Second World War on that estate in Wakefield, but I can still vividly recall the sense of unified purpose from those days. The doors were open for children like me, thanks to the spirit of fairness that lifted a determined Britain and its citizens out of the hardship brought down by the war years.

Opportunities and possibilities seemed to lie almost tangibly in front of us. We felt that if we did well, we could get on – whether that meant going to Oxford, as I did, or going into high-status, well-paid work, like many of my school friends. The term 'social mobility' had yet to be coined, but that was what we were seeing, all around us. It was the golden age of social mobility. The promise of those immediate post-war years, and the possibility of re-awakening that promise, was very much the inspiration for my work with the Sutton Trust.

Many decades later and here we are, in the middle of a new kind of war, this time against a deadly virus. The enemy is wholly different, but the challenges are the same: poverty, unemployment, families struggling to put food on the table. And for many children of lockdown, potentially lasting damage has been dealt to their chances of forging successful careers once they leave school. Having fallen behind in the pandemic, they risk falling behind for good, losing not just a few months of their childhoods, but a lifetime of opportunity.

The crisis itself will pass. Even as I write this, the headlines are full of encouraging news about vaccines. But what of the damage it will leave? The spirit that informed the rebuilding of Britain after 1945 – the idea that government, individuals and civil society must unite to create a safety net to protect all of us, throughout our lives – will be exactly what we need again to ensure that people and the country can prosper beyond this crisis. We need a national effort for the twenty-first century to ensure no one is left behind.

What does this look like? It starts by recognizing that this country fails to give every young person a fair crack of the whip and pledging to change that. It starts from a determination to halt and reverse the decline of social mobility – to restore the ladders to success which were in place for previous generations like mine, but whose rungs have been allowed to rot and fall away.

Why is it that in 2020, children from poorer backgrounds are less likely than comfortably-off children to get access to good schools and to go on to the best universities? Why is it that entry to many top jobs – whether it's law, medicine, fashion, film – so often depends on being supported enough to be able to undertake an unpaid internship? Why is it that our world-leading public schools can't work with government to make places available to smart kids from low- and middle-income backgrounds, who couldn't possibly pay fees? And what sense does it make to talk about social progress when a kid living today in the house I grew up in has less chance of getting to a top university now than I did in the 1950s?

The pandemic, and the reconstruction of our society that it will necessitate, obliges us to ask these questions again, and with new energy and purpose. Life doesn't have to be tilted at every stage against those who have the least to begin with. Putting this right is not impossible. Indeed, it's a project well suited to those great human qualities often alleged to be intrinsically British: common sense and fair play. Those qualities come together in the exercise of entrepreneurial philanthropy – the approach to social giving that I have tried to set out along the way in this book. In the wake of the global pandemic of 2020 and the damage it has dealt, both immediately and in the longer term, the call for entrepreneurial philanthropy – the act of stepping up to help others step up – goes out again now, yet even louder.

ACKNOWLEDGEMENTS

Firstly, I'd like to express my love for my family, to whom this book is dedicated.

I'd also like to thank my friends who have made my life so enjoyable over the years.

A company and a trust are by definition a team endeavour. I'd like to thank everyone who worked with me at the Sutton Company and the Sutton Trust, and others who have made those places so successful and so much fun to be a part of.

Finally, I'd like to thank Giles Smith for being so great to work with and for doing such a wonderful job.

Thank you everyone.